Grannie Annie, Vol. 13

Historical Family Stories from
The Grannie Annie Family Story Celebration
Written and Illustrated by Young People

Saint Louis, Missouri

The Grannie Annie
Family Story Celebration

Welcome to the 2017/2018 Grannie Annie celebration of family stories! Students in U.S. grades 4 through 8, and homeschooled or international students 9 through 14 years of age, are invited to interview their family storykeepers and write a story from their family's history. The Grannie Annie experience leads young people to strengthen family and community bonds, encounter history in a personal way, and polish their writing skills. Students are encouraged to illustrate their story and then share their work with their family, school, community, and The Grannie Annie.

The works of thirty-five young authors and ten young artists, chosen to represent the submissions received this year, are included in this thirteenth annual volume of *Grannie Annie*. This year's stories are available in eBook, PDF, and paperback editions, and are also published on The Grannie Annie's website and through social media.

The Grannie Annie mission — to inspire young people to discover, write, illustrate, and share historical family stories — springs from a belief in the transformative power of "story." The simple, genuine family stories in this book can help us connect with people in today's world and with people from times past. In unexplainable ways, these stories foster feelings of unity with people whose lives may seem very different from our own. Quietly, surely, the world moves one step closer to peace.

Published by The Grannie Annie Family Story Celebration, P.O. Box 11343, Saint Louis, Missouri 63105.

The Grannie Annie welcomes — and desires to receive and publish — family stories from students of every race, ethnicity, national origin, religion, and creed.

Because the stories in *Grannie Annie, Vol. 13*, were captured from the oral tradition, they represent a unique blend of history, legend, and opinion. Accuracy — historical or otherwise — is not guaranteed, and the views represented are not necessarily those of the authors, directors, or publishers.

Cover illustration by Janessa Hoffmann.

Particular thanks to fiber artist Elda Miller, and graphics specialists TJ Jerrod, Josh Hagan, and Jeff Hirsch.

Financial assistance for this project has been provided by the Chester D. and Elda F. Miller Foundation, Anne Perkins, Louise and Jack McIntyre, and other generous donors.

Anthology copyright © 2018 by The Grannie Annie Family Story Celebration. All rights reserved with this exception: Individual stories may be copied for classroom use, or by the authors and illustrators as noted, who also retain the copyrights to their works, printed here with permission. If you wish to include one or more of the stories in a publication (print, electronic, or otherwise), you must contact The Grannie Annie Family Story Celebration for permission, and you must give attribution to the individual author(s) and/or artist(s) and to The Grannie Annie Family Story Celebration. If you have questions regarding your right to share these stories, please contact The Grannie Annie Family Story Celebration.

Publisher's Cataloging-in-Publication Data
    Grannie Annie : selections from the Grannie Annie family story celebration, an annual writing and illustrating opportunity for young people.

    p. cm.
    (Grannie Annie ; vol. 13)
    ISBN 978-0-9969394-3-0

1. Oral biography. 2. Family history. 3. Family—Anecdotes.
4. Older people—Interviews. 5. Grandparents—Anecdotes.
6. Family folklore.

HQ518 .G72 2018
920—dc22   2008204710

In memory of
Ann Guirreri Cutler,
whose passion for saving family stories
inspired The Grannie Annie
1944–2007

* * *

In memory of
Anne H. Desmond,
1933–2018.
We shared each other's stories
and became close and beloved friends.

Honored by donor Anne Perkins

* * *

In honor of our family
and all the stories we've shared—
our 6 children and their spouses,
24 grandchildren and spouses,
29 great-grandchildren,
and those yet to come.

Honored by donors Louise and Jack McIntyre

Contents

The Grannie Annie Family Story Celebration

Copyright and Acknowledgments

Dedications

Story Settings Map, International

Story Settings Map, United States

A Word from Grannie Annie

Note to Parents and Educators

  1. Bloody Hill (August 10, 1861*) by Aidan McCoy; Missouri, USA

  2. Outlaw Uncle (1870s) by Rylan Dickens; North Carolina, USA

  3. Can't I Go to School? (c. 1905) by Noa Temima Harris; New York, USA

  4. Lucky on the *Lusitania* (1914, 1915) by Claire Lewis; North Carolina, USA

  5. The Backyard Coaster (c. 1938) by Ilonka Guilliams; Missouri, USA

  6. Love at First Sight (1939) by Bella Pagano; Missouri, USA

  7. A Single Ring (1939) by Emily Mark; New York, USA

  8. A Personal Situation (December 7, 1941) by Alex Newman; Missouri, USA

---

* The time setting of each story is noted in parentheses here and also on the story pages. Where the exact year is unknown, "c." (circa) indicates the approximate year.

9. The Flying Messengers of World War II (c. 1942) by Emma Miller; Missouri, USA

10. The Man in Stripes (1940s) by Chavy Reiss; New York, USA

11. Kindness in Darkness (1944) by Malka Lavner; New York, USA

12. The Day My Grandma Learned to Pick Up Her Toys (c. 1945) by Julia Martin; Missouri, USA

13. Let Us Not Forget (c. 1945) by Ivy Slen; Missouri, USA

14. To Live (1948) by Rami Kessock; New York, USA

15. Importance of Rainwater (c. 1951) by Brock Bowman; Missouri, USA

16. Help (1951) by Piper Shepard; Nebraska, USA

17. A Wrong Turn (1955) by Elizabeth Clawson; Missouri, USA

18. Pocket Alarm (1963) by Jaden Johnson; Colorado, USA

19. Sammy's Rough Road Trip (1966) by Isabel Draper; Missouri, USA

20. A Tough Decision (c. 1969) by Tyler Hott; Missouri, USA

21. The Lunar Rock Legacy (1969, 2010) by Anagi Pieris; Missouri, USA

22. Two Friends Meet Up After Thirty Years! (1971, 2001) by Mary Neal Cheek; North Carolina, USA

23. Hard Work Down the Drain (Almost) (c. 1973) by Tien Le; North Carolina, USA

24. SOS – Saving Our Sand Dune (1973–1975) by Carolista Walsh; North Carolina, USA

25. My Mom and the Monkey (c. 1975) by Ava Hornburg; Missouri, USA

26. The Worst Pet Ever (c. 1980) by Owen Reinsch; Missouri, USA

27. How a Bull Taught Me How to Shave (c. 1980) by Elsa Whitney Sawyer Walz; Ohio, USA

28. The Tornado (c. 1980) by Ethan Wienstroer; Missouri, USA

29. The No Good Terrible Very Bad Day (1981) by Taylor Lim; Missouri, USA

30. Candy Thieves (1981) by Ella Munz; Missouri, USA

31. Grandfather, the Swimmer (1983) by Ameer Jawad; Missouri, USA

32. The Note in the Cowbell (1985) by Kate Bohlmann; Missouri, USA

33. Where's the Cake? (1985) by Lucy Abbott Fader; North Carolina, USA

34. The Chocolate Chip Cookies (c. 1989) by Avery Johnson; North Carolina, USA

35. Dine and Dash (c. 1991) by Cadence Andrus; Idaho, USA

Illustrators of *Volume 13*

Invitation to Participate

Grannie Annie Storykeepers 2018 and Their Story Titles

Praise for The Grannie Annie

Story Settings Map, International

Numbers on map are story numbers.

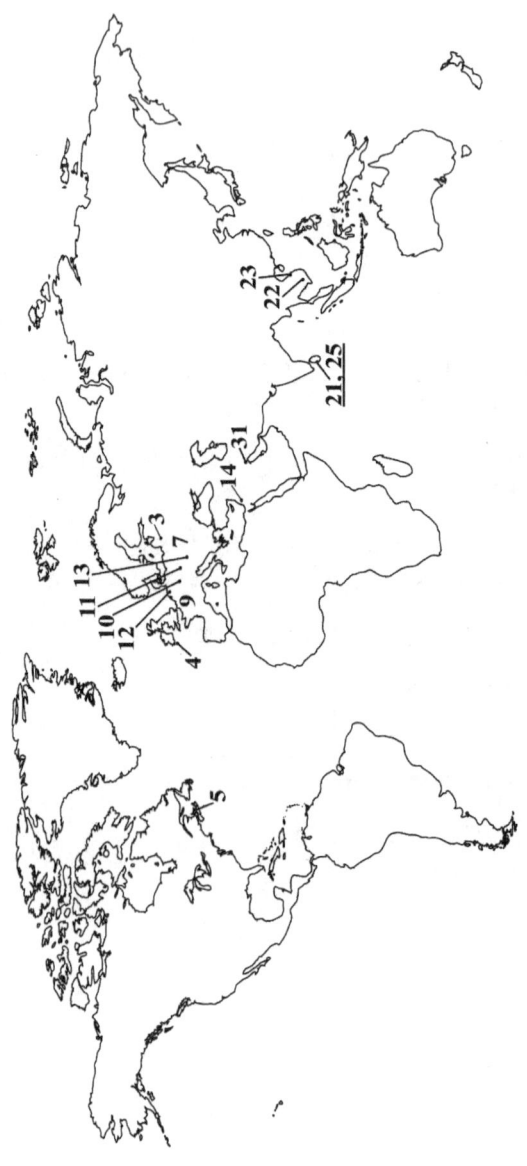

Story Settings Map, United States

Numbers on map are story numbers.

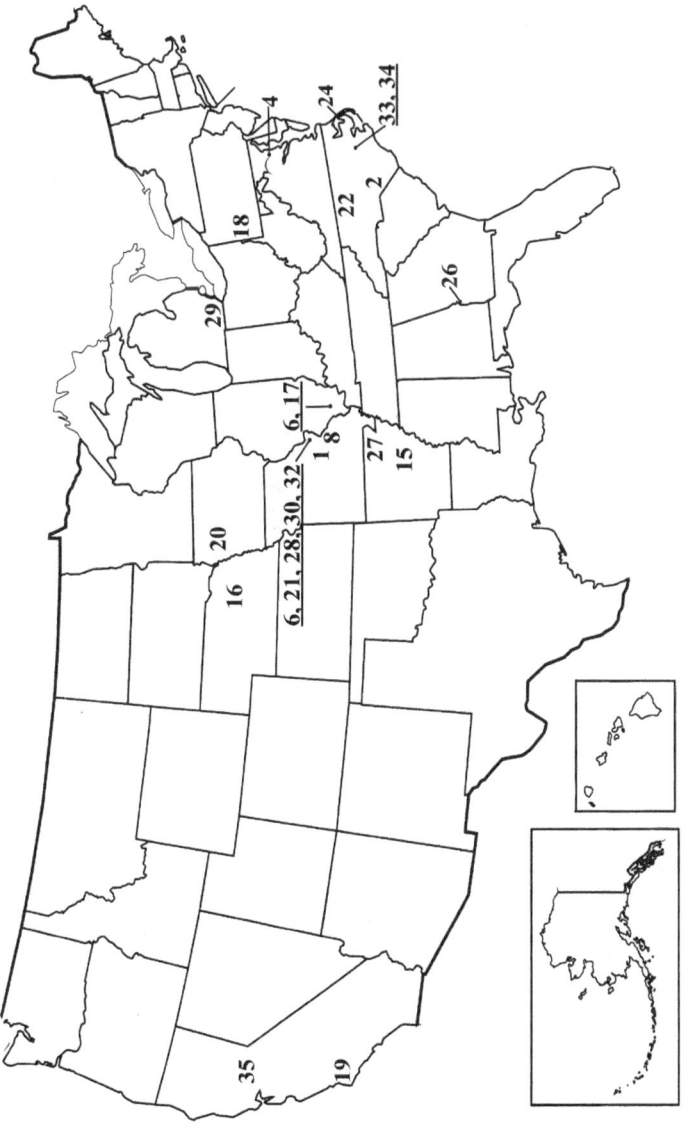

A Word from Grannie Annie

Some Native American nations so valued their histories that they designated a tribal storykeeper. My mother filled that role in our family for decades, and before that, our family storykeeper was Mom's mother, my grandmother Randazzo.

Gramma Randazzo lived with us when I was a child. She didn't speak English well; however, at an early age I learned to say "Tell me a story about the Old Country" or "Tell me again the story about the baker's daughter who had dough under her fingernails." Then she would begin, in her broken English that made the stories even more fascinating to me. She told me stories about the olive groves on the family estate in Italy, about Grampa Randazzo's brothers and all their escapades, and about the family's early years as immigrants in Brooklyn. Mom carried on the tradition with her own repertoire of stories — about teaching in a one-room school, about blizzards and floods on the farm, and about rolling up the rug and inviting the neighbors over to dance.

I was fascinated by their tales and still am. I have written down many of their stories, saved them in keepsake books so they won't be lost. They're a treasure to read now, just as I had hoped, but I find I saved more than the stories themselves. Listening had been a way to be close to Gramma Randazzo. When I read Gramma's stories now, I remember sitting near her, hearing the stories from Gramma herself. When I read Mom's stories now, I remember aunts and uncles and cousins gathering around the kitchen table to listen. By sharing their stories, Gramma and Mom created a sense of family, a sense of closeness and security, that will stay with me forever.

Ann Guirreri Cutler, The Original Grannie Annie, April 2006

Note to Parents and Educators

You're invited to watch an American Civil War battle from your front porch, then journey by ship and train, on a school bus and in a lonely camper trailer — even in a junk-yard cart — through the inviting pages of *Grannie Annie, Vol. 13*. You'll visit ten states and thirteen countries, and meet everything from surprise to despair to unbelievable kindness.

You won't be alone. You'll be traveling with some of the bravest and most imaginative family members around — standing up to slavery and bulldozers, and standing up for us all by carrying a coal bucket; planning a narrow escape and planning a thrilling date. There will be questions along the way: When is it okay to cry? When is it okay to run?

There's a chance you might sink or swim. Or you might be dancing in the street or singing with the radio and then *BAM!* You might decide to live every day, for love.

So much entertainment, education, and inspiration in this one small book! It's a hopscotch trip through the 528 priceless stories shared with The Grannie Annie this year. Our volunteer readers chose the stories in this collection with your family in mind, yet you may want to preview them before sharing them with young or sensitive readers.

We're so pleased that you've joined us, and we hope you'll travel with us again next year through The Grannie Annie Family Story Celebration!

Connie McIntyre and Fran Hamilton, Directors of The Grannie Annie

Listening is an act of love.

—Dave Isay, StoryCorps

Grannie Annie, Vol. 13

1.
Bloody Hill

August 10, 1861;[1] Oak Hill, Missouri, USA

My name is Olivina Ray. Most people call me Olivia, and I'm six years old. I was not frightened by the Civil War at all, but after the battle on Bloody Hill, my mind changed.

One day I was playing with my six siblings on the porch, and suddenly a soldier marched up the yard and shouted at me. "Git the heck inside. There's gonna be a battle, and we're takin' over your land!" he barked with an accent. More soldiers were behind him, preparing for the battle of their lives. Most of the children scrambled into the cellar, but I managed to stay upstairs with the adults and all the chaos.

The house was crowded enough when there weren't soldiers around, but now they turned our humble home into a medical center with soldiers crawling around every inch. I got to see the battle from our front porch while sitting on my grandpa's favorite rocking chair. I saw movement in the corn, but I didn't tell anyone.

The soldier that yelled at me before found me and my grandpa, escorted us to the cellar door, and pushed us hard into safety. It was loud outside because of the gunfire, cannons, and men wailing, but in the cellar those noises were amplified! I couldn't sleep or think. It looked like my grandpa couldn't either. We'd had enough.

When all was quiet, Grandpa slowly climbed up the ladder and opened the hatch. First one foot, then the other — he swiftly stepped out. *Ka-POW!* A cannonball struck the ground, barely missing Grandpa's feet! The force was so strong he slid down the ladder, hitting every rung on the way, and bruised his head. That was the end of curiosity for him.

When my family finally came up from the cellar five days later, most of our crops were trampled. There was blood — there were dead and injured soldiers — everywhere. It was the worst sight I ever saw in my life.

I slid down the slippery hill towards the corn and saw someone alive. It was General Nathaniel Lyon! My family hauled a wagon down to him, and soldiers wheeled him to our house. That's where he stayed until he passed away later that night.[2]

The Battle of Wilson's Creek, also known as the Battle of Oak Hills, was fought near Springfield, Missouri, on my family's property, on August 10, 1861. This is the story of my great-great-great-aunt Olivia Ray, who saw the battle with her own eyes. My family would later sell this property to the government for the greater good.

Aidan McCoy; Missouri, USA

1. The setting of each story is noted below its title. In cases where the exact year isn't known, "c." (circa) indicates that the year given is approximate.

2. General Nathaniel Lyon was the first Union (Northern) general to be killed in the American Civil War.

2.
Outlaw Uncle

1870s; Robeson County, North Carolina, USA

Who would have thought that I had a real-life Robin Hood, or outlaw wanted by the law, in my family history — someone who is often written about in history books today?

I didn't know much about my Lumbee Indian heritage until I interviewed my mom, Jamee Dickens. Due to my grandmother's dementia, this story reflects what my mom remembers her mom and grandmother telling her about this wonderful Indian legend. My mom took out the family tree to show me how the story relates to our family.

My grandmother grew up in Robeson County, North Carolina. She is a Lumbee Indian. The Indians of Robeson County all know the local history of the Indian warrior named Henry Berry Lowry. He was known as a hero to the Indian people — just like the spectacular hero Daniel Boone. My mom reports that there are some restaurants and businesses in Robeson County that still portray his picture with his story today.

Henry Berry Lowry was known for his role in waging the war against slavery of the Indian people. He was born in 1845, and was my mother's great-great-grandmother's uncle. My mom showed me this on the family tree and discussed some of the challenges that the Indians faced. They experienced many differences from the white people. My grandmother was born in 1935. She had to sit separate from the whites and drink from different water fountains and attend Indian-only schools. My grandfather, who was white, was not even allowed to marry my grandmother in 1957 in North Carolina, because she was Indian. They had to go to South Carolina to marry.

I learned that slavery was an issue for the Indians of North Carolina. However, the Indian people were not thought of as "good" slaves like the African-Americans. My mom tells me that even the Tuscarora War of 1711 was about this very thing. Even as late as the hectic Civil War, attempts were made to try to enslave Indians. The Indians were often referred to as "Negro."

It was Henry Berry Lowry who, after the Civil War, took a stand against slavery, becoming an outlaw with a price on his head, laying his life out on the line for his Indian people to have freedoms. It was shortly after one of his most daring raids, in which he robbed a local sheriff's office safe of $28,000, that he disappeared. There are conflicting reports of how he truly died. It is thought that he accidentally shot and killed himself while cleaning his double-barrel shotgun.

Since 1976, Henry Berry Lowry's magnificent adventure has been portrayed in the Robeson County musical outdoor play called *Strike at the Wind!* It presents Lowry's legend during the Civil War and depicts Lowry as an outlaw hero fighting for his people's rights.

I am proud to have learned of this wonderful piece of history that my family shares.

Rylan Dickens; North Carolina, USA

3.
Can't I Go to School?

c. 1905; Slabodka, Kaunas, Lithuania

My great-grandmother Gittel Lipshits was a smart seven-year-old girl. Her mother was dead, and her father worked as a rabbi in America; therefore, Gittel lived with her uncle in the town of Slabodka, in the suburb of Kovno, in the country of Lithuania. Unfortunately there was a rule — a wicked, cruel rule — a rule that girls could not go to school.

How boring it must have been to spend every day at home helping your mother with chores. There were upsides though — no tests, no homework. It was like never-ending vacation. But Gittel was smart — and infuriated. Unlike most, she *wanted* to go to school — badly.

"I want to go to school!" Gittel whined to her uncle for the umpteenth time.

"I have said this already, Gittel. You can't. Go find something to do," her uncle replied.

Yet Gittel still thought she could find a way to go to school. She thought about it. And an idea came.

"Of course! Why didn't I think of this before? The rabbi!" Gittel thought. Any regular seven-year-old going to the great adult rabbi would probably be terrified. What could happen? For all she knew (and she knew a lot), the rabbi would be busy. "What if, like everybody else, he'll say no?" she thought bitterly. But she went.

And the rabbi thought about the situation. Gittel waited.

But soon the rabbi said, "How about this? You could become coal girl for the local schoolhouse. While you do your job, you can listen and learn. Does that sound good?"

"Brilliant!" Gittel sang. And so she became the coal girl.

Every day Gittel would walk to the one-room schoolhouse. Her job was to sit by the furnace and make the fire stay warm, and in between caring for the dancing flames she could lie back and listen to what the teacher would say. Gittel was glad she had gone to the amazing rabbi.

Later on, she was able to go to school and learn properly. She grew up to be a great woman.

This story is important to me because it reminds me of the phrase "Where there's a will, there's a way." And if I'm stuck in a situation like my great-grandmother was, I'll remember there's always a solution and a way out.

Noa Temima Harris; New York, USA

4.
Lucky on the *Lusitania*

1914, off the southern coast of Ireland; 1915, Washington, D.C., USA

On May 8, 1915, my great-great-grandmother Laura Powell despaired when she sat down to drink her steaming morning tea and read *The Washington Post*'s headline: "Steamer *Lusitania* Torpedoed and Sunk off Irish Coast."

Seven months earlier, on October 3, 1914, Laura Powell had boarded that same ship near her birthplace in Liverpool, England, to make the weeklong transatlantic journey to New York to be with her soon-to-wed fiancé, Arthur. World War I had begun two months earlier, and German U-boats[1] had just started to patrol the treacherous water around England. Laura surely didn't know what was to come on her voyage across the Atlantic Ocean.

Not long after her journey began, Captain Daniel Dow made a terrifying statement over the ship's loudspeaker while Laura was getting dressed. There was, in fact, a German submarine chasing them! All of the passengers, including Laura, were petrified. Immediately everyone started to cover the portholes with cloth so that it would be more difficult for the submarine to determine the ship's exact location. When it came time for dinner, all of the fine china was gone! The crew had stored it away so that passengers wouldn't accidentally drop something and make a horrific sound. All of the cooking supplies were put away, so passengers had to eat sandwiches and colder fare off of paper plates. On the way back to their staterooms, the men, women, and children had to walk very quietly, as if they were mice, because the captain didn't want the German submarine to hear them.

Eventually — on October 9, 1914 — the *Lusitania* safely reached the American shoreline at Ellis Island, near New York City. My great-great-grandmother was greeted by her family, and they went home to Washington, D.C.

They were all devastated just a few months later to learn that the *Lusitania* had been sunk by a German torpedo. Several family members had sailed on the *Lusitania* over the years as they traveled between their homeland of England and the United States.

The passengers and crew of the *Lusitania* had almost made it back to England on the voyage! The ship was sunk off the coast of Ireland, just before reaching her final destination of Liverpool. Maybe the torpedo had been fired from the same German submarine that had been following the *Lusitania* when my great-great-grandmother was aboard. Approximately 1,198 people died on that fateful day in May. It was then that my great-great-grandmother realized that her voyage on the *Lusitania* had been a lucky one!

Claire Lewis; North Carolina, USA

---

1. "U-boat" is short for *Unterseeboot*, German for "undersea boat." The term refers especially to submarines used by the German military during World Wars I and II.

5.
The Backyard Coaster

c. 1938; Pictou, Nova Scotia, Canada

It was the summer of 1938, and my grandma Patricia was one of eight siblings. She had six brothers and one sister; she was the youngest girl in the family. Her brothers were always getting into trouble and pulling jokes on each other. The last trick they pulled led to a close call.

One day my grandma's brothers made a goal to find trouble. As they were walking home, they found an open dump, where they stumbled across an old conveyor rail, wheels, and other pieces. They all knew this was going to be fun, and they had a plan for what to do with the rails. In the backyard of their home was the steepest, meanest hill you would ever see. The brothers smiled a mischievous smile.

They began to build their coaster. At the top of the hill, they pieced the rails together like a track going down the hill. Then they dashed to the garage to get the wagon they had built from the rusty spare parts, and they placed it on the track. It fit.

Now they were ready, and the oldest boy, Joseph, asked proudly, "Who's gonna try it?"

Everyone was smart enough to not try anything the boys had made. No one said anything. The only one who had no clue what was going on was the third-youngest boy, Bernard. Joseph snatched Bernard and convinced him to ride the wagon.

Bernard grinned. He liked the idea of being the bravest and knew he would now be included in the group, so he agreed to ride. He plopped himself into the raggedy cart. Smiling the biggest smile in the world, he wiggled and jumped in the cart. Joseph stepped back and gave the wagon a big push.

The old rusty cart gave way. It rolled vigorously down the steep hill. As it got going faster and faster, Bernard finally understood why no one else wanted to ride in the wagon. He felt a small bump, and before you could *snap*, he was in the middle of a busy street.

With his hands sweating, his heart pounding, and his face red, he screamed in rage and fear. He had trusted his siblings' coaster when he really shouldn't have. The cart zoomed past loud cars that were honking at him. He could hear muffled voices in the background, and everything seemed to slow down for a second. A loud honk rang in his ear and broke the silence.

There was another bump, but this time it was much larger than the earlier bump. This one was enough to launch him, and that's just what happened. Paralyzed by terror, he flew up in the air but somehow stayed in the cart, which hit the hard cement bricks of the house across the street.

My grandma's father stepped out to see Bernard, scratched and bruised, walking up the hill with the wagon. Since Bernard wasn't really injured; his parents were more worried than angry.

You can still see the chip in the house to this day. The siblings got in some trouble for their antics, and they all learned to think before acting.

Ilonka Guilliams; Missouri, USA

6.
Love at First Sight

1939; Herrin, Illinois, and St. Louis, Missouri, USA

Angelina and Pauline had been friends since childhood. One day Angelina, who had moved to Illinois, decided to visit her friend Pauline in St. Louis. Richard, Angelina's nephew, drove her more than one hundred miles to see her best friend, for she could not drive. Rich saw Pauline's daughter, Josephine, and fell in love at first sight.

When Rich got home, he decided to send Josephine a gift, without consulting anyone about the proper etiquette. Rich chose a very expensive brush, mirror, and comb set. In St. Louis, Josephine received her gift in the mail and got in huge trouble. Back then, boys did not send gifts to girls, and it was frowned upon.

The following day Pauline, beside herself with confusion, called Angelina to set a date to figure things out. Angelina hastily called Rich to see if he could come over. Unbeknownst to him, he was in for a long, and very loud, lecture over the proper behavior for young men.

Rich and Angelina again drove two hours to St. Louis to see Pauline and her daughter to make things right. Angelina and Pauline interrogated Rich and Josephine with questions of "What did you do?" and "Why did you do it?" filling the air with loud voices. Rich explained that he sent the extravagant gift only because he wanted to show Josephine that he liked her. Angelina and Pauline laughed, thinking how incredible this was, for the two young people had never been alone and had barely talked. Finally, after Josephine and Rich begged them, Pauline and Angelina set the ground rules for the young people's first date. They decided to go to the movies.

Smushed in the car, shoulder to shoulder, Rich, Josephine, Angelina, Pauline, both of their husbands, Josephine's grandma, her two sisters, brother, aunt, and uncle all accompanied them as chaperones to the movies. Rich bought popcorn for Josephine and, not wanting to be rude, emptied his wallet and got it for everyone.

Everyone walked into the theater, "politely" asking a few people to leave their seats for the large group, who took up an entire row. Entering the now-empty row, Rich went first, followed by everyone but Josephine, going last. Sitting on opposite ends of the row, they awkwardly leaned back as the movie began.

A few months later my great-grandparents, Rich and Josephine, were married. They had known each other for only a short time, but they knew that they would be together forever. Rich and Josephine were married for fifty-five years, until Josephine passed away in March 1994. They had three children, their two boys being my grandpa and uncle Joe, and their one girl being my aunt Amalia.

Rich's gift to Josephine continues to travel throughout my family, going from generation to generation. At this time, that brush, mirror, and comb set is sitting on my sister's dresser. This is a treasured family heirloom that my sister and I look forward to passing along to our children.

Bella Pagano; Missouri, USA

7.
A Single Ring

1939; Sokal, Galicia, Poland[1]

It was 1939, and much of Europe had just entered World War II, which included the Holocaust. The Germans, having taken control of parts of northern Europe, rounded up Jews from Poland, Germany, and surrounding areas. The Germans took the Jews to concentration camps, death camps, or gas chambers. My great-grandmother Hanna Steichel was forcibly taken on a train to a concentration camp.

Hanna and her parents, Sarah and Aryeh, herded onto a cramped cattle-car train, were headed to a concentration camp. Sarah spotted a crack in the train floorboards. The cattle car slowed as it rounded a bend in the track, and Hanna's parents begged her to squeeze through the crack so she could escape. It was risky and dangerous. If she were spotted in an attempt to escape, she would surely be killed.

Scared and unwilling to part from her parents, she cried, "No! I won't leave you!" Her parents knew this was her only chance for survival. In an act of pure selflessness, Hanna's mother pushed her through the crack in the floorboard, saving her life at the expense of their own.

Having been squeezed through the floorboards, Hanna was released from the train. The tracks were raised on a platform, and as she was freed, she tumbled down a gully. As the train straightened out in its path, it picked up speed. Hanna ran into the nearby forest and hid among the trees for two weeks, surviving on rainwater and berries.

While in the woods, Hanna found a ring engraved with the initials "MK." Having no physical possessions left to her name, she kept the ring and placed it safely in the pocket of her dress.

Two weeks seemed like a lifetime to a scared and cold Hanna. After wandering the dark, cold woods, searching for suitable hiding places and food to survive, Hanna found a convent tucked away deep in the woods.

Seeking shelter at the convent, Hanna explained she was a war refugee. Hanna pleaded with the nuns to allow her to shelter with them in exchange for her cleaning the convent.

Nazi troops, who were searching for hidden Jews, came through the convent, accusing Hanna of being a Jew.

"No, I'm not," she fearfully answered.

The Nazi officer accused her of lying and backhanded her, knocking a tooth out. She reached into her pocket, taking out the ring she had found earlier in the woods. "My name is Maria Kostas," she trembled, explaining that "Maria" is a Catholic name. Believing her, the Nazi officer let her be.

I am thankful for that little ring that saved my great-grandmother's life, for it is because of that ring that I am here today.

Sometimes a little thing can make a big difference.

Emily Mark; New York, USA

Illustrator: Jasmine Flowers; Missouri, USA

1. Sokal is now part of Ukraine.

8.
A Personal Situation

December 7, 1941; Bloomsdale, Missouri, USA

Have you ever got into a position that got personal fast? My great-grandpa happened to get into just such a personal situation. It was December 7, 1941, and my great-grandpa was thirteen. He had a school play, but before the play started, my great-grandpa decided to go to the outhouse. This trip to the outhouse was going to be like no other.

As my great-grandpa walked up the stairs, he noticed a man — a man Great-Grandpa thought he had never seen before. The man was average height with his shoulders bent down, his hands on his head, and his back slouched down.

When my great-grandpa got all the way up the stairs, he could tell this man was his school bus driver. My great-grandpa saw a tear in his bus driver's eye. This made my great-grandpa's hands sweaty, and butterflies danced in his stomach. Great-Grandpa was uncomfortable, because he was used to seeing his bus driver happy. My great-grandpa had never seen a man cry before in his thirteen years.

The bus driver had twelve kids — ten boys and two girls — and all ten boys were in the service. My great-grandpa asked the bus driver what was wrong. The bus driver told my great-grandpa that Pearl Harbor had been bombed by the Japanese earlier that day. Standing in awe, my great-grandpa asked why the bus driver was so upset. The bus driver said two of his sons were in Pearl Harbor, and he didn't know if those two sons were alive. With abundant tears streaming down his face, the bus driver asked my great-grandpa not to tell anyone, and my great-grandpa promised.

The next morning on the way to school, my great-grandpa ran down the aisle of the bus to ask the bus driver if his sons were okay. The bus driver said that earlier that morning he had received a call from the army. The army said both sons were alive and uninjured. My great-grandpa was delighted with this great news. The whole day after that, my great-grandpa couldn't stop thinking about the bus driver, his sons, and Pearl Harbor.

Alex Newman; Missouri, USA

9.
The Flying Messengers of World War II

c. 1942; eight countries in Europe, including England, Ireland, and France

At the age of twelve, young Richard Kasak came home from church and found a pigeon with a broken wing. His father cut a hole in the top of a chicken coop and placed a box in the coop with the pigeon inside it. In no time, other pigeons came around, because Richard offered food and shelter for the wandering birds. He fed them and cared for them for several years. Caring for the pigeons became his hobby and filled much spare time.

When he got drafted into the U.S. Army, Richard was told he would be a radio operator, but he had to test to see what he was best at. He was really good at marksmanship, but marksmen were more likely to die than other people. So Richard purposely did poorly at the marksmanship test so he wouldn't have to be a marksman. The army decided he was best at carpentry and had him do that for a while. He drove trucks and built outhouses at all of the new places.

Richard learned somehow that the U.S. Army Air Corps[1] was creating an experimental unit of 125 men who had experience with pigeons. At first he thought it was a joke, but he was intrigued, so he signed up for this project.

He had to go to training first. Then he had to learn how to teach the pigeons to remember a path and deliver messages from one site to another. There was an 18-foot by 18-foot platform with a hole in the middle that held feed and water. The men set the pigeons in the middle and let them loose. When the pigeons were hungry, they would return to eat. Every three or four days the men would move the platform — beginning with 3 feet, then 100 feet, followed by half a mile, and eventually 18 miles or more. At some point a second platform with feed and water was introduced so that pigeons would learn to fly to more than one place.

After the pigeons were trained, they were taken to the front lines. From there, they carried capsules on their legs with messages in code, saying the soldiers needed supplies or other help. Richard's unit, called the 277th Signal Pigeon Company, would pass the messages along to people who would get soldiers the supplies or other help they needed.

My great-grandpa Richard Kasak says he didn't do much in the war — even though he helped send important messages that saved many lives and helped win battles.

Emma Miller; Missouri, USA

1. The U.S. Army Air Corps was the part of the U.S. Army that handled aviation. It became the U.S. Air Force in 1947.

10.
The Man in Stripes

1940s; Germany

In the 1940s during World War II my great-grandfather Zaidy,[1] who was twenty-one years old at the time, was torn apart from his family, and ended up in a concentration camp in Germany. He didn't know where his family members were, what they were doing, or if they were even alive. He felt devastated, miserable, and all alone.

Zaidy and his fellow inmates were given the job of cleaning up after Allied[2] bomb attacks on the trains. The Germans didn't give them any food, since they were expected to scavenge the ruins and find food for themselves. This was a dangerous and tough job, but also partially rewarding, because Zaidy and his friends actually got to see how the Allies were destroying the German trains and tracks.

One sunny day Zaidy was cleaning up with the rest of his group when all of a sudden he saw hundreds of bomber planes every fifty feet or so. The Allies were dropping a row of many bombs at a time, and they were inching closer and closer to him and his friends.

Zaidy was starting to get really scared and nervous, when suddenly he came up with a plan. Instead of trying to outrun the planes like most would do, especially when they're panicking, he told his friends to run in the direction opposite of the way the planes were headed. This way they would be in an area where the bombs had already been exploded. Unfortunately some of his friends didn't listen to his idea, and sadly, they ended up dying. The ones that listened to him survived.

After the bombs were dropped and exploded, the Allies took out machine guns and tried to kill the rest of the people that didn't die. One plane was specifically going after my great-grandpa. Zaidy quickly hid in a bomb crater, but then noticed that the plane could shoot him from the other side. He was petrified and frightened, yet knew that he had tried his best. When the plane flew closer, the pilot must have seen Zaidy's striped clothes and realized he was a prisoner. In the last second the plane turned away, and Zaidy couldn't believe his eyes.

The moral of this story is that even in your absolute worst moments don't panic and give up all of your hope. If not for my great-grandpa's courage and bravery, I wouldn't be here to tell this story today.

Chavy Reiss; New York, USA

1. "Zaidy" is Yiddish for "grandpa."

2. The Allied forces were the twenty-six countries, including Great Britain, the United States, France, and the Soviet Union (USSR), that fought against Germany, Japan, and other countries in World War II.

11.
Kindness in Darkness

1944; Langenbielau labor camp, Bielawa, Poland

Have you ever been in a hard situation? Or maybe had to decide if you should help someone or not? In the Holocaust this would come up a lot. My great-grandmother Sala Lencher was a Holocaust survivor.

It was 1944, and my great-grandmother was in a labor camp. The people in the camp had to sew uniforms for the Nazis. At the time, Sala was eighteen. But there was a problem. Sala did not know how to sew. Her friend told her that she would sew for Sala. This was putting both their lives in danger. Sala told the Nazis she could sew. My great-grandmother was very grateful to her friend. Sala was a fast learner and quickly caught on. (Later she sewed all her children's clothing. I still have a stuffed dog she sewed for my mother.)

Time passed, and Sala met the factory foreman's wife. The factory foreman's wife was kind to Sala and grew very fond of her. One day the factory foreman's wife pointed to her desk and said to Sala, "In my drawer every day I will put a piece of bread." She continued, "You may take it." This was putting both their lives in danger.

"Thank you!" Sala was very grateful. This was a huge help, because there was never enough to eat. The next day Sala took her extra piece of bread. But instead of eating the whole piece, she split it with her friend who had taught her to sew. Later on, she said she had never even thought to eat it all herself!

Afterwards the factory foreman's wife offered to adopt Sala. This was very kind, because Sala did not know if she had family who had survived.

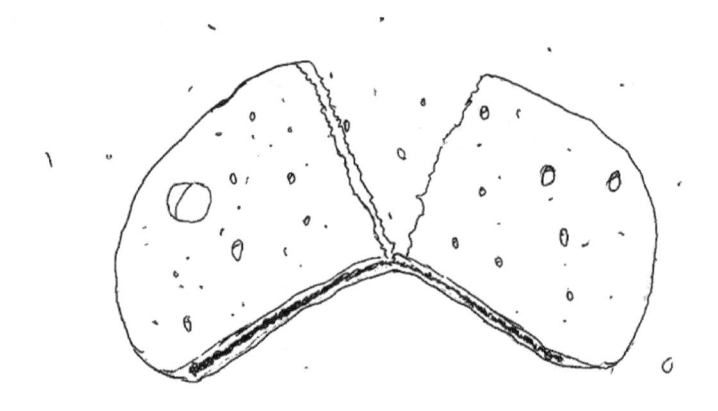

Sala was once again grateful but responded, "I am so sorry, but I cannot leave the Jewish nation. I must remain loyal to my family, and committed to the Jews."

When the Holocaust ended, Sala went to find her family. She had started out with seven siblings, but sadly only three had survived. Her parents had not survived either. She moved with her siblings, Rachella, Ada, and Yisrael, whom they called "Srulic." Sala got married and had my grandmother Malka and my great-uncle Yaakov.

I learnt from my great-grandmother to always care about others, even if you are in a bad situation.

Malka Lavner; New York, USA

Illustrator: Cameron Churchich; Colorado, USA

12.
The Day My Grandma Learned to Pick Up Her Toys

c. 1945; Onstwedde, the Netherlands

A young girl named Wina and her friend came together to play outside one day in Onstwedde, the Netherlands. Wina found a jump rope and tied it to a bar on a gate. She and her friend took turns skipping rope, happily forgetting the silent street and the cruel war that was keeping their country hostage. Suddenly the girls stopped playing and stood, listening, for they were sure they heard a noise come from further down the street.

The sound became clearer and louder than before. The girls soon realized that this mysterious sound wasn't an uncommon one. Looking down the street, they saw a threatening column of German soldiers solemnly led by a Nazi officer proudly riding on horseback. The soldiers were marching in strict formation right towards the little girls.

Terrified, Wina and her friend sprinted to the friend's house as fast as they could, for they knew well that German soldiers were ruthless and dangerous. When they were in the house, out of sight, they hid, shaking with fear by a window. Secretly and noiselessly they watched and waited with bated breath as a German soldier on horseback stopped his horse and looked down at the jump rope. The girls watched even more intently as he suddenly bent down, untied Wina's jump rope from the gate and, without looking back, took it on horseback!

After the soldiers were safely out of sight, Wina and her friend ran back outside, devastated that their favorite plaything was gone. They looked at each other and became angry, for that was their rope! Afterwards, with heavy hearts, they both grudgingly decided that from then on, they would take their toys with them whenever they would go inside.

Years later that little girl named Wina immigrated to America and became my grandma. Even now, at an older age, she remembers that frightening moment. She still wishes she and her friend had taken the jump rope inside with them that day. As a result, she still is very persistent in keeping a clean house all the time.

Julia Martin; Missouri, USA

13.
Let Us Not Forget

c. 1945; between Buchenwald concentration camp (central Germany) and southern Poland

My great-grandpa Fred Slen was a prisoner during World War II because he was Jewish. At the beginning of the war, he was just seventeen. He was put in a concentration camp, and his entire family was murdered by the Nazis. He endured a forced march between camps, where all he had to eat was raw potatoes that he dug up with his own hands, and he had to squeeze rainwater out of his hat so he could drink. He survived the war living in a concentration camp with very harsh conditions.

Toward the end of the war, when my great-grandfather was about twenty, he was put on a train in a cattle car with the other surviving Jews from his death camp. One of his good friends, Joe, was with him on the train. The Nazis were moving the prisoners away from the front lines, because they were trying to hide them from the Americans. After a while the train stopped, and the doors of the train were opened. The Nazis announced to the prisoners that they were free to leave if they wanted. Many people started to run into the nearby woods and the fields to be free.

My great-grandpa did not trust the Nazis and did not move a muscle.

Joe was about to run out of the train with the others when Fred held him back by the arm and pleaded, "Don't go. It's a trick!"

Thankfully Joe considered my great-grandpa's request, because a few seconds later the Nazis opened fire with machine guns and killed all the people who had run from the train.

My great-grandfather saved his best friend's life that day — and his own! The boys hugged as the Nazis closed the doors of the train and continued down the track to another camp, where Joe and Fred lived out the remainder of the war in horribly harsh conditions.

When the war was over, both Joe and Fred had survived and were liberated by the Americans. They remained the closest of friends for the rest of their lives.

It is my job as a descendent of Holocaust survivors to tell this story for generations to come so tragedies like this won't happen again. Let us not forget!

Ivy Slen; Missouri, USA

14.
To Live

1948; Jerusalem, Israel

On May 14, 1948, Nachman Ofer was spiritedly cheering and dancing in the streets with the rest of his Jerusalem neighbors and family. He was seven years old, and Israel had just officially become a state. Nachman had two older sisters and an older brother named Yitzchak. His mother, Chava, was pregnant with a baby boy, and his grandfather lived in an apartment across the street. Nachman had a very sharp memory and was in a school for gifted children. As he waved his new Israeli flag, Nachman could not imagine any place he would rather be.

In 1934 Nachman's father, Ephraim Dov, had moved from Lublin, Poland, to the land that would become Israel. His father's brothers, who were still in Poland, had been killed in the Holocaust. Nachman's father became a construction worker and traveled all over Israel building houses. After Israel became a state, Nachman saw his father less and less frequently. The neighboring Arab countries had attacked, and his father was busy building trenches and fortifications to be safe from Arab snipers.

On the morning of June 11, 1948, Nachman and his family were relieved to hear that there was a ceasefire between Israel and its Arab neighbors. Their home had been hit hard by the shelling, and they'd already had to move homes once. Nachman left with his father and brother, Yitzchak, to go to synagogue while things were still calm.

Just then they heard a deafening boom, and Ephraim Dov collapsed. Yitzchak shouted at Nachman, "Take Mother inside!" because she had fainted from shock.

As Nachman dragged his mother indoors, he heard more shelling outside. His heart was pounding like a hammer. He ran back outside to check on his father. His neighborhood was destroyed, his grandfather was injured, and his brother was standing over his father's dead body. His father had been killed instantly.

Life changed very quickly for Nachman. His mother gave birth to a baby boy, and named him after her husband, Ephraim Dov. She couldn't afford to keep all her children, so she sent Yitzchak and Nachman to live in an orphanage. There were many crying, traumatized children living there, so Nachman never got much sleep. He was not fed well either, so he and Yitzchak scavenged food from grocery trucks. Nachman had to leave his school, and lost almost three years of education. During that time Chava opened up a grocery store, and finally earned enough money for Yitzchak and Nachman to return home.

Today Nachman Ofer, my great-grandfather, lives in New York. He and his wife, Rachel, have four children, fourteen grandchildren, and nine great-grandchildren.

Nachman learned early that one day you could have everything you'd ever want, and the next day it could all be taken from you. He tries to live every day as if it is his last.

Rami Kessock; New York, USA

15.
Importance of Rainwater

c. 1951; Humnoke, Arkansas, USA

Have you ever wondered how guilt changes life? Here's an example.

My grandpa — "Pap," as we call him — was about five years old when this story took place. Pap was with his seven-year-old cousin, Tommy. They were making a road in the dirt driveway, using rocks to line the roadway and empty bottles for their cars.

Then some hens came with their chicks and scratched up their newly built road. The boys were furious! So they put the chicks in a five-gallon bucket and moved them to the shady backyard.

The boys worked hard and rebuilt the road. Just as they started playing with their bottle-cars, the chicks returned and scratched up the road, obliterating the boys' roadway yet again. The boys were explosively angry!

They gathered the chicks and once again took them to the backyard. This time the boys decided to not take any more risk of having their roadway destroyed, and chose to once and for all fix their problem. They smashed the heads of the chicks with bricks and got rid of them for good by dumping the little chick bodies into the barrel for rainwater. The boys returned to their play and rebuilt their roadway just the way they liked it.

Tommy's mom, Florency, came home from picking blackberries and found the dead chicks in her rainwater. The boys wisely sensed Florency's anger and hid under the house. Florency called for them, but they did not respond. So she baked a blackberry cobbler in order to lure them out of hiding.

The boys smelled the cobbler and decided Florency must not really care about the chicks, and they came out to eat. Once they went into the kitchen, they quickly realized this was a bad decision. Between them and the door stood Aunt Florency with a leather belt.

After their punishment, Florency fed the boys some cobbler and listened to their side of the story. She then explained that she was more upset about the rainwater being ruined than about the death of all the chicks. Rainwater was important for many things around the house.

The guilt the boys carried from this event changed their lives. Tommy became a preacher and baptized people instead of chickens. My pap chose to raise chickens as pets and watered them with rainwater that he collected in a five-gallon bucket.

Brock Bowman; Missouri, USA

Illustrator: Cecelia Vannoy; Missouri, USA

16.
Help

1951; Greeley, Nebraska, USA

It was a cold Friday evening in November 1951. I was looking at a Christmas catalog in the dining room while my little brother, Mick, was playing with his trucks under the kitchen table. As usual, my father was sitting in his chair, reading the weekly newspaper, and my mother was in the kitchen putting away supper. My sister, Mary, was sitting on the couch looking at the fireplace when we heard the kitchen door slam open.

BANG! I heard a gunshot, my mother's scream, and a crash from a fallen glass milk container. My father and I scrambled to our feet and ran into the kitchen.

Standing in the doorway was a man I didn't know, but I knew he lived close by. I had seen him a few times. He had shot my mother in the shoulder! My father yelled at me to run to the closest neighbor's house.

I went through the alfalfa field next to our house. Since we went to school that way, I was familiar enough with the field to go through it in the dark. Next I crossed the train tracks and then the country road to the neighbor's yard. The neighbors were not there, so I turned on a light and called the party line,[1] hoping my aunt would answer the phone.

"Hello?" my aunt said. I was happy to hear her voice. I told my aunt what had happened, that I was terrified, and where I was. My aunt just told me to keep calm and stay in the house until I could hear the ambulance and police. I was okay with that. I turned the lights back off and sat in the dark in the old house, scared and worried, for a while. Soon I heard an ambulance and the police, and felt a little better knowing there was help coming.

I started back home. I was still a little scared, but who wouldn't be? When I was almost home, my father met me halfway through the alfalfa field and said, "Hurry up! We have to go to Grand Island with your mother." I ran back with him.

My mother was in the hospital for several months.

When my mother was finally allowed to come home, she had a ball she was supposed to squeeze to get some of her strength back into her arm, but she didn't use it. Instead of squeezing the ball, my mother decided to peel apples to get her strength back. My mother was one tough woman.

The man who had shot my mother was in a mental hospital for a while. After the incident, we got a phone since we hadn't had one before, but we barely used the phone again.

My great-grandmother was a very strong woman, and I wish I could have met her. This story was told by my great-aunt Jean, who is now seventy-five years old and can still tell this story full of details and from her heart.

Piper Shepard; Nebraska, USA

1. A party line is a telephone line shared by several customers. Each customer has a unique ring code. When any customer on the line is called, all the phones on the line ring that customer's ring, and any or all customers on the line can answer the call.

17.
A Wrong Turn

1955: Marion, Illinois, USA

Getting lost can be a frightening thing, but when you happen to meet something even more frightening on the way is when things start to get really scary.

In the summer of 1955 my grandma Phyllis was eight years old. She lived in southern Illinois in a small town called Marion. One time her mom had to visit a friend in Chicago, and she needed someone to watch Phyllis while she was gone, since Phyllis's dad worked.

Phyllis ended up staying with her aunt Christine and her husband. They lived in the rural country with their four children. The front of Aunt Christine's house faced a road. The other sides of the house overlooked acres and acres of cornfields.

One sunny morning Phyllis and her cousins decided to play in the fields. They strolled out the back door and into the corn. The five lively kids looked and looked until eventually they discovered a bare spot, where they plopped themselves down. After a little while they wanted some old pots and pans to play with. Phyllis volunteered to go back to the house to fetch them.

Phyllis couldn't see over the tall green stalks, and she crossed row after row until she figured that she had somehow passed the house. She was as scared and lost as could be. "I'll never get out!" she thought to herself while crying. She finally decided to follow one row all the way, because this would have to lead her somewhere eventually. She started running.

Aunt Christine had a neighbor far down the road to the right who happened to keep a very large bull in their pasture. Well, Phyllis ran and ran until she came face to face with that bull. His fur was brown and white, and matted all over. Huge horns grew from the top of his head, and from his nose hung a big golden ring. "Humph," the bull puffed.

Phyllis felt his hot breath against her face. The bull stood motionless in a pen at the time, but his head hung over. Phyllis was completely terrified. She pondered to herself, "If this bull is to the right of the house, then if I turn around and continue on, I'll come to Aunt Christine's house." She took off and ran as fast, and as far away from that bull, as possible.

After what seemed like half a day of sprinting, Phyllis burst out right on the side of Aunt Christine's house! She was extremely overjoyed to finally be back again, but everyone else was standing there looking so distraught. They had been searching high and low, but no one could find her. And here she was!

When looking back now, Phyllis laughs, though she admits the experience seemed horrible at the time. She definitely learned something and, though silly, the lesson is important: Don't ever go into acres of cornfields when the corn is way over your head, and especially when you're only an eight-year-old girl.

Elizabeth Clawson; Missouri, USA

Illustrator: Yuka Iwasawa; Missouri, USA

18.
Pocket Alarm

1963; Pittsburgh, Pennsylvania, USA

I loved rock music. My parents had just bought a transistor radio. Since cell phones had not been invented yet, it was the only means of handheld communication. I loved to listen to music on it. I would take it to school and listen to it in the boys' restroom, even though it was not allowed. We would all sit in the bathroom listening to the little radio.

One day I took the radio to school to listen to music in the bathroom like any other day. I'd listen to it and go back to class. Later on in the day during social studies I was dying to hear some music. I went up to our teacher, Mr. Beares, and asked if I could go to the bathroom.

"Yes, but hurry back," Mr. Beares said.

"I will," I replied.

Once in the bathroom, I turned on the radio. It buzzed — then music started playing. But for some reason the music stopped. The radio crackled. For a second I thought some little thing had gone wrong with the radio, but I was very wrong. The problem was not — and I mean *not* — small.

"We bring you this special report," said the radio. "President John F. Kennedy has been shot in a motorcade in Dallas, Texas."

My heart sank. Our great, and probably best-looking, president had been shot. I ran back to my classroom, and as soon as I was in it I ran to Mr. Beares's desk.

"JFK got shot," I said.

"How do you know?" asked Mr. Beares.

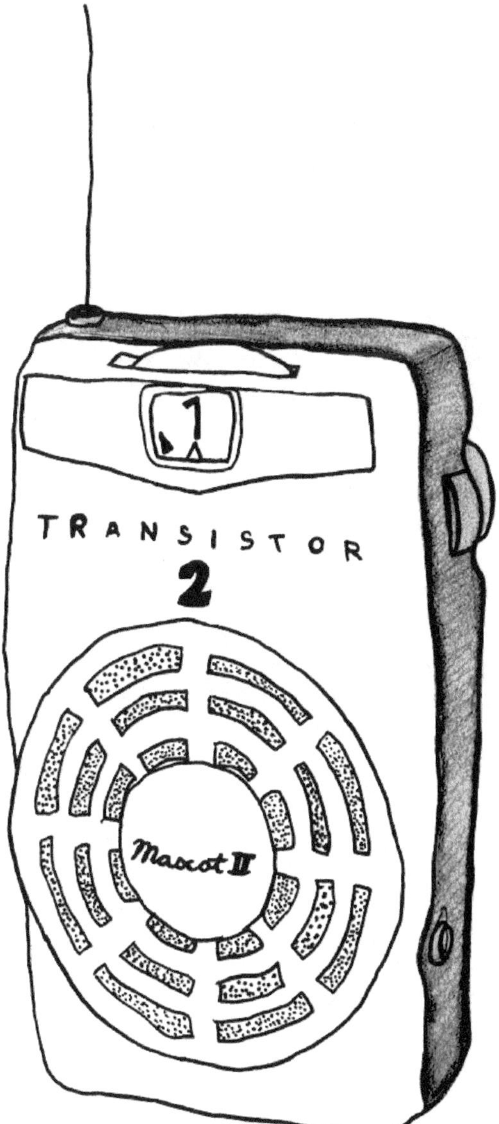
TRANSISTOR
2
Maxcot II

I slowly pulled the radio out of my pocket.

"Well, turn it up so we all can hear!"

That was a terrible day in America.

Jaden Johnson, grandson of the narrator of the story; Colorado, USA
Illustrator: Devyn Shelton; Missouri, USA

19.
Sammy's Rough Road Trip

1966; Lompoc, California, USA

Dogs are odd. Some love the car, and some get sick just seeing it. No matter what dog, they all hate one thing — being alone.

It was spring in 1966 on Vandenberg Air Force Base. Lucius and Ginny Draper, my grandparents, had bought a camper trailer for their trip to Massachusetts that summer. They wanted to test the camper, so they planned to go on a weekend camping trip with their three kids and their two dogs.

With some hassle, Ginny and Lucius herded almost-three-year-old Sandra, five-and-a-half-year-old David, and eight-year-old Bruce into their sedan. Sammy, their twenty-five-pound mostly black mutt, would travel in the camper. Feller, their four-month-old not-quite-trustworthy puppy, would ride in the car. They started driving down the road.

After about an hour, they checked on Sammy, who was fast asleep. Bruce, David, and Sandra, who were antsy from being in the car, woke Sammy up, which proved to be an awful mistake. After ensuring Sammy was comfortable, the Drapers got back in the car and started driving again. Sammy saw his people in his car, driving away. He wanted to go, too. He scratched at the curtains. He wanted to catch his people. He scratched harder at the door. It opened, swinging in the breeze. Sammy jumped.

In the car, everything was going smoothly. They were almost at the crest of a hill on a two-lane road. A couple passed them. On a two-lane road, this is a crazy time to pass, because a car could come over the hill and *BAM!* — there would be an accident. The lady in the car yelled out her window as they drove by, "Your dog fell out of the trailer!" Ginny pressed the brakes after confirming with Lucius that the lady had really said their dog fell out of the camper. Ginny swerved onto the side of the road, and Lucius got out of the car.

The camper door was shut, but the camper was empty. Lucius disappeared into the dust. Ten suspenseful minutes later, he came back, clutching Sammy to his chest. Sammy's paws were scraped, his nose was pink and bleeding badly, and he was missing a couple of teeth. Lucius and Sammy got back in the car, with everyone rejoicing that Sammy was alive. The family drove to the vet to fix up their beloved pet.

Sammy's scrapes and nose healed. He made many more trips with his family in the trailer, but he never went inside the trailer unless his people were already inside. And he was never the last to leave.

Did Sammy jump because he thought he was being left behind? Maybe he was simply lonely. Whatever the reason, my family is grateful for the lady who risked her life to tell them Sammy was gone. Without her, Sammy could have died on the road, or starved to death.

If it is possible, help others.

Isabel Draper; Missouri, USA

Illustrator: Janessa Hoffmann; Missouri, USA

20.
A Tough Decision

c. 1969; Lake View, Iowa, USA

Everyone at some point in their life has received a call from their mother that makes their adrenaline start to run. However, some calls are more serious than others.

The year was 1969 in the city of Lake View, Iowa, and all was going well. My grandma Doris had been dating Bill, her boyfriend, for what seemed like an eternity. However, Bill was a Catholic, and Doris was a Lutheran. Doris's family was not happy with this.

Doris and Bill were becoming more and more serious in their relationship throughout the year. Doris was constantly wondering when Bill would propose to her, and when she would be able to start her own family with her beautiful, outstanding husband. She was excited, and she had everything in her life that she could ever want.

That evening Doris could hear the phone ringing when she was two rooms away, in the basement. She swiftly dashed up the creaky wooden stairs and into the living room, where the phone was ringing. She uncoiled the twisted wire and nudged the phone toward her ear. She was thrilled that it was her mother calling, because she hadn't talked to her in forever.

However, Doris's mother was not happy. She was furious, in fact. Her mother could sense that the relationship between Bill and Doris was growing stronger and stronger, and her mother did not want her amazing daughter to marry a Catholic man. Then her mom announced to her own daughter that if she were to marry the Catholic man, the rest of the family would ditch Doris and would never talk to her or see her again.

Doris had the choice either to stay with Bill and never see her family again, or to dump Bill and stay with her family.

She pondered over the decision for a while, and she went where her heart was. She would marry Bill.

To this day they are still a happy married couple, and Doris has noticed someone in her family only once — because they ran into each other at a grocery store.

Doris is glad that she pursued her heart, even though it was a hard decision. Without her nerve-racking call, I would never have been alive and my dad would never have existed. Even though Doris is no longer able to see her family, she is still delighted with her choice and that she followed her gut.

Tyler Hott; Missouri, USA

21.
The Lunar Rock Legacy

1969, Gampaha, Western Province, Sri Lanka;[1] and 2010, St. Louis, Missouri, USA

Everyone has moments from their childhood when they were carefree and innocent. It might have been their ecstatic delight in discovering an anthill, or the nurturing care with which a toddler regards his pansy. All families share these treasured moments from their golden years, during which they romped blithely. Dad's escapades with his brother are Pieris household classics.

In one of those tales, six-year-old Dad was already demonstrating his legal advocacy skills by convincing his younger brother to accompany him in a doomed pastime. This occurred when the USA was emerging victorious in the Cold War. The world waited with bated breath as Apollo 11 landed men on the moon on July 20, 1969. It was a historic moment for the United States and for the world, as the first humans left their mark on extraterrestrial soil.

Soon after their pioneering mission, the three U.S. astronauts went on a world tour. My father was born in Sri Lanka, which was among the countries Neil Armstrong, Buzz Aldrin, and Michael Collins visited.

Dad's family resided in an old house that my great-great-grandfather built for his family in what was then a sleepy hamlet called Gampaha. Their home was next to the railway station. The three astronauts traveled by train in Sri Lanka, and my father recalls racing towards the station with his five-year-old brother, Alex Mama (Uncle), to see those great men who had walked on the moon. Dad was ecstatic to see them in person. As the locomotive slowed down, Neil Armstrong and

Buzz Aldrin waved at the cheering crowd on the platform. Daddy was in a giddy mood, so he and Alex Mama practiced being astronauts.

No one remembers exactly what happened, but being a boy, Dad managed to wedge a stone up one of his nostrils! A young boy who abruptly finds his sense of smell diminishing would certainly panic. However, Shantha J. Pieris — Dad — was different. He was under the impression that Atcha, his mother, could fix anything. Imagine Atcha's horror when she discovered the stone was stuck. The mischievous boy was escorted to the hospital, where the doctors painstakingly extricated the gifted "moon rock." Later, Alex Mama mimicked Dad's feat by wedging a rock in his ear! Atcha was not amused.

For these reasons, for my family the lunar landing is remembered with great fondness. Forty years later, history repeated itself when Mom urgently contacted Dad at work to address a domestic crisis! My two-year-old brother, Avunker, had spontaneously stuck a bead up *his* nose. Fortunately, Dad made him sneeze it out with pepper.

Despite barriers like age, maturity, and homeland, my brother eerily mimicked Dad. Regardless of the factors that would have set them apart, two significantly different people identified. Even if a person immediately perceives another as fundamentally different from themselves, remember we all have funny childhood stories or troubles to share — all that's required is a listening ear.

Anagi Pieris; Missouri, USA

1. In 1969 Sri Lanka was called "Ceylon."

22.
Two Friends Meet Up After Thirty Years!

1971, Thu Cuong, South Vietnam;[1] 2001, Greensboro, North Carolina, USA

My grandfather wasn't with my mom when she was born. He was halfway across the world fighting in the Vietnam War. It was 1971. During his first week, my grandfather was in a patrol boat. One boat caught on fire, and in the confusion two boats ran into each other, and my grandfather fell into the water. A man name Bich[2] pulled him out of the water. They became fast friends. Every night they sat by the water or played volleyball. The closer they became, the more my grandfather learned from Bich. My grandfather said that every time Bich talked about how Vietnam would have freedom, he had this fire in his eyes.

When my grandfather's baby's due date was near, he stayed off river patrol. The American radio communication had strict orders to find him when the word was received that the baby had been born.

On July 9, 1971, Bich came running up to my grandfather with tears of joy in his eyes, telling him he had a new daughter. A few minutes later a crowd of people came to tell my grandfather he had a new daughter. Bich had found out first, because he had set up his own radio. Bich had the honor of choosing a Vietnamese name for my mom. My grandfather and grandmother named her Joan, and "Loan" was the closest Bich could get in Vietnamese.

Six months later my grandfather's yearlong tour of duty was over. He returned to the United States. My grandfather tried to keep up with Bich, but he stopped getting letters from him. My grandfather was afraid his friend had died.

More than twenty years later, Bich and his wife were on a cruise to China. They met a United States Navy officer. Bich told him about my grandfather. The officer found my grandfather on the Internet. Bich wrote a letter to him.

Two weeks later my grandfather flew out to California to see Bich. Then my grandfather invited Bich and his wife for my mom's thirtieth birthday. On July 8 they arrived in North Carolina for her birthday.

My grandfather said, "I didn't think I'd ever see him again." Since then, Bich and my grandfather have had lots of visits.

Bich became a United States citizen in 1991. We take our freedom for granted, but Bich did not. As my grandfather has said, "Freedom is the greatest gift of all."

Mary Neal Cheek; North Carolina, USA

1. In 1976, after having fought each other in a war, North Vietnam and South Vietnam were merged to form one country: Vietnam.

2. "Bich" rhymes with "pick."

23.
Hard Work Down the Drain (Almost)

c. 1973; Da Nang, South Vietnam[1]

In 1973 my dad lived in Vietnam. He was in the seventh grade and needed a bike, but he didn't have enough money to buy one. My dad had to buy individual parts of a bike and put them together to make a new one.

Every week, my dad would go to the flea market and buy bike parts. He bought pieces like the handlebars, chains, pedals, etc. He gathered up all of the pieces except for the frame, which he had to get from a separate bike store. When he earned enough money to buy the frame, my dad put the receipt and the serial number the frame came with in the hollow seat post. Once he got home, my dad painted the frame a pale blue.

After he put together the bike, my dad rode it to school in the mornings and home from school in the afternoons. One day he came out from the school building and couldn't find his bike. He looked everywhere, but it was nowhere in sight. When he thought he had lost it or someone had stolen it, he went to the principal's office to report his missing bike.

When he walked in, the principal was holding my dad's bike with another boy standing next to him. The boy claimed my dad had stolen *his* bike and repainted the frame. My dad was very agitated, upset, and confused, because the boy was lying.

Then my dad remembered that he had put the receipt in the seat post. He borrowed a few tools and got it out. He showed the receipt to his principal and finally got his bike back. He rode home, relieved that he remembered where he had put the receipt.

My dad was also very *proud* that he remembered where he had put the receipt — and that he had even thought of putting it in the seat post in the first place.

Tien Le; North Carolina, USA

Illustrator: Miles Montgomery O'Dwyer; Missouri, USA

1. In 1976 North Vietnam and South Vietnam were merged to form one country: Vietnam.

24.
SOS – Saving Our Sand Dune

1973–1975; Nags Head, North Carolina, USA

This is the story of how my grandma Carolista, whom I am named after, risked her life to save the largest sand dune on the East Coast.

The year was 1973 in Nags Head, North Carolina. Nags Head was a small vacation town on the Outer Banks[1] with few stores and few year-round residents. My mom, Inglis, who was five, and her siblings, were playing on a big sand dune that everyone called "Jockey's Ridge," directly across from their house. It was quite normal for them to be playing on the dune, since it was just across the road, but what was about to happen wouldn't be normal at all.

As the kids and their babysitter headed back to the cottage, they saw a bulldozer at the foot of Jockey's Ridge bulldozing small dunes. Worried about their sand dune, they sprinted back to the house to call their mom, Carolista, to tell her.

Upset after hearing the news, Carolista quickly left her store, Carolista Jewelry Designs, picked up her kids, and scurried across the street to Jockey's Ridge. She then marched up to the bulldozer operator, and she didn't ask but she *told* him to stop bulldozing the dunes. She then proceeded to stand in front of the bulldozer, which could crush her at any given moment, and refused to move.

The standoff between the two seemed to last for an eternity, but it was probably just a few minutes until the operator hopped off his bulldozer defeated, and left. After he left, Carolista pulled off the distributor cap so the bulldozer wouldn't start.

Carolista called Jim Hunt, the North Carolina governor, begging him to find funding to save Jockey's Ridge. The governor, moved by Carolista's enthusiasm and determination, obtained an injunction to stop the process of building the condominiums. The state agreed that if they got enough money, they would buy Jockey's Ridge and preserve it as a natural landmark.

Carolista then set out with the goal of making Jockey's Ridge a state park. Her thought was "This land belongs to the people," because it is so unique and special. She started raising funds by selling T-shirts and bumper stickers in a booth that sat at the foot of the dune — and even "selling square feet" of Jockey's Ridge for five dollars apiece. Between the contributions from donors, and state grants, enough money was raised to purchase the property. On May 31, 1975, Jockey's Ridge was preserved as a state park forever! It is now one of the top three most visited state parks in North Carolina, with over 1.3 million visitors per year.

Sadly, this incredible, unstoppable woman died when my mom was only twenty, which is sad for my mom, me, and everyone who got the chance to get to know this powerhouse of a person. I wish with all my might that I could have met her. Even though Carolista has passed, she left an amazing legacy and, of course, the sand dune she worked so hard to save.

Carolista Walsh; North Carolina, USA

Illustrator: Janessa Hoffmann; Missouri, USA

1. The Outer Banks is a string of sandy islands and peninsulas running parallel to the coast of North Carolina and southern Virginia.

25.
My Mom and the Monkey

c. 1975; Angoda, Central Province, Sri Lanka

My mother grew up in a convent located in Sri Lanka, which is a small tropical island nation off of the southeast coast of India. The culture and customs were different from those in America. Monkeys were common pets like cats and dogs. At the time, my mother went by the name of "Nishanthi." She was a curious and naughty child.

Her older sister, Vasanthi, was the complete opposite. She was a shy and timid girl. Vasanthi always tried to keep her younger sister out of trouble. They lived in Sri Lanka until 1980, and this story took place in the mid 1970s.

The two sisters lived in the convent because they had been abandoned by their parents. There was a kind family who had been a neighbor of their parents, who often had the sisters over on school breaks.

One day Nishanthi and Vasanthi were invited over to the family's house for lunch. When playing in the backyard, Nishanthi noticed that they had a pet monkey. Their monkey was tied to a chain. "I wonder what would happen if I poked the monkey with a stick," said Nishanthi.

"Nishanthi, don't poke the monkey," said Vasanthi.

Unfortunately, Nishanthi decided to poke the monkey. Vasanthi hid in the house out of fear. Nishanthi shoved the monkey many times, and it started to get annoyed. The monkey broke from the chain in anger and chased Nishanthi into the house. The monkey ended up devouring all of their lunch and wrecking the family's kitchen. Vasanthi cried because she knew that Nishanthi was going to be in a great deal of trouble.

All the adults were outraged at the monkey. However, Vasanthi told them what Nishanthi had done, because she was fearful and did not like to lie. The adults were furious at Nishanthi, and she got severely punished.

We can all learn many lessons from this story. The most significant is that we should think before we act. This is always crucial to remember, because when we think, we sometimes stop ourselves from making mistakes. When my mom didn't think, she ended up getting chased by a monkey and getting into much trouble. Even though this same thing probably would not happen in America, this story can demonstrate many lessons that we can apply to our own lives.

Ava Hornburg; Missouri, USA

26.
The Worst Pet Ever

c. 1980; Fort Benning, Georgia, USA

Have you ever wanted a pet as a child? Well, so did my mom. My mom, Jennifer, was just six years old, and all that she wanted was a pet, but her parents constantly told her no. But one day my mom was surprised by a gift from her dad.

As the head of a poor family, my mom's dad had to hunt for their food. On a frigid winter day my grandpa said he was going to "get a deer." When my mom heard her dad was going to "get a deer," she was so excited! My six-year-old mom mistakenly thought she was going to have a real live deer, the greatest pet ever! My mom could not wait to tell all her friends at school about the amazing pet she was going to have.

My grandpa set out with his neighbor, ready to "get a deer." Through the trees my grandpa spotted a deer emerging into sight. My grandpa motioned to his neighbor to look at the deer. My grandpa took a shot at the deer and watched the deer fall, lifeless, to the ground. Below the trees was the dead deer.

When Grandpa returned home, his neighbor helped him skin the deer and hang it on my mom's swing set. When Grandpa went back inside, he said he "had a deer."

My mom dashed outside. She could not wait to play with her new pet. Standing in awe, Mom gazed at the dead deer. Blood dripped from the bottom of the dead deer onto my mom's swing set. Mom screamed and cried like a newborn baby, tears falling from her cheeks. Mom sprinted inside and shoved her head into her pillow. Her parents uselessly tried to soothe her. My six-year-old mom learned that if her parents say no, then she should just let it go.

Even though my mom wanted a pet, she never expected a pet like that! A few years later my mom did get a dog but had to get rid of it a few months later. My mom still gets upset about what happened that day, but she still loves animals.

Owen Reinsch; Missouri, USA

27.
How a Bull Taught Me How to Shave

c. 1980; Calamine, Arkansas, USA

As a boy growing up in Arkansas, my pawpa Sawyer spent a lot of time with his mawmaw and pawpaw Milligan at the old home place. So on a vacation, he wanted my grandma to see the old home place he had talked about so much. They left my mom, as a baby, with her great-uncle so they could hike out to see the now-falling-down house on the other side of a field.

As they were walking towards the place where my great-great-grandparents once lived, they were talking about Pawpa's memories of the old house, when they heard a sniff and a grunt. They looked up and saw a **BIG BLACK BULL** coming towards them! They had known that there was a bull, but they had never seen it before and had not ever hoped to see it!

As the bull was coming towards them, they had to race to the crumbling shelter. They hoped the bull would forget about them if they disappeared from sight. Outside, a storm came quick; luckily the bull wandered away to look for a dry spot.

As my pawpa stood under the leaning roof to wait out the rain, he told my grandma that his pawpaw used to shave out on the front porch. As a boy, my pawpa would get water from the cistern, in a cup, and then he was allowed to use the horsehair brush to lather the soap. He then acted out the steps he remembered seeing his pawpaw do. "He would stand right here," he showed my grandma. "Pawpaw would reach up over his head and pull his shave kit from the porch rafters." And then Pawpa did the very same thing! Seventeen years after his grandpa had died, from the porch of the crumbling house, he held in his hand his pawpaw Milligan's straight-razor kit.

My grandparents still have Pawpaw Milligan's shave kit from the old home, and they both think that it was left there for my pawpa to find.

When I spend the night at my pawpa's house, in the morning he lets me sit up on the bathroom counter, he puts shave cream on his face, and I get to help him shave. I am glad that big black bull was there to chase Pawpa and my grandma into the house so my pawpa could think about watching his pawpaw shaving. I'm pretty sure that bull is why I know how to shave!

Elsa Whitney Sawyer Walz; Ohio, USA

Illustrator: Lawson Holestine; Missouri USA

28.
The Tornado

c. 1980; Hazelwood, Missouri, USA

Everybody knows how you're supposed to go inside and stay in a safe place during a tornado. There was one time when my uncle Andy didn't, and he learned his lesson when a tornado came. My mom's (Christy's) parents were out for their anniversary. Helen and Andy, my mom's teenage sister and brother, were outside hanging out with their friends in the yard.

Then my mom heard on TV that there was a tornado coming. She put her little brother, Scott, to bed in the basement, then went outside to tell Helen, Andy, and their friends to come inside because a tornado was coming. When she told them to come inside, they called her a "goody two shoes." She tried to get them to listen, but it was futile.

The wind started to blow and howl like crazy. That is when Helen, Helen's friend, and Andy's friends decided to go in. Andy decided to stay outside. When Helen and her friend opened the front door, it ripped off its hinges and flew off, spinning like a piece of paper in the wind.

Andy thought the stick fort he and his friends had made would protect him. Then all of a sudden the black swirling, howling whirlwind picked up the stick fort with Andy in it and slammed it back down to the ground. Andy ran to the jungle gym and held on for dear life. The wind from the monstrous tornado blew Andy around like a flag in a tornado. Even with the intense winds blowing him around, he still held on. Finally Andy was able to get on the ground and run inside, even with the strong winds.

After he got inside, he went down to the basement. My mom, Helen, and their friends were so glad to see Andy in safety with no severe injuries. Until the tornado was gone, they didn't leave the basement. Meanwhile the tornado continued to cause destruction outside. It smashed up the shed in the yard and scattered the pieces everywhere.

A while later the tornado stopped, but it left a mess. The good news was that the house was fine. When my mom's parents got home, they found the front door ripped off. They didn't know there had been a tornado, because it didn't strike where they were. They found pieces of the shed a few blocks away.

From that experience, Andy learned the lesson that you should always go inside during a tornado.

Ethan Wienstroer; Missouri, USA

Illustrator: Walker Brand; Missouri, USA

29.
The No Good Terrible Very Bad Day

1981; Deerfield, Michigan, USA

When my mom was in kindergarten, she rode the school bus home every day. (When my mom was younger, she was really, really shy.) Her house was the farthest away from the school. Her normal bus driver was really nice, but one day the normal driver was sick and there was a substitute bus driver.

One by one, all the kids got dropped off the bus, including my mom's best friend, Heather. Then my mom started to worry. When the substitute bus driver got to my mom's house, she just drove by — *Vroom!* The bus went straight past her house — it didn't slow down, not even a bit! My mom was *petrified*! She kept as quiet as possible, and huddled in the corner of her seat.

The bus driver drove back to school, got off the bus, and came back with a broom to clean the bus. *Swish, swash.* Side to side the broom went. The bus driver looked from seat to seat, checking for trash. When the bus driver got to the very last seat, she saw a little kindergartner huddled in the seat. And just like any bus driver should do when they see a kid on the bus, she screamed. Then my mom uncurled herself and started screaming, too!

The bus driver calmed herself and asked my mom in a strict voice, "Why are you still on the bus, little missy?"

My mom said squeakily, "You passed my house."

The bus driver was startled, so she took my mom to the school office and told the secretary, "This girl got left on the school bus. Can we call her mom?"

So they called my mom's mom, but she did not hear the phone because she was outside waiting for the bus and the phone was inside. The secretary called one more time, and my mom's mom still did not pick up. My mom was trying so hard not to cry. Nobody wants to cry in front of an adult, unless it's their parents.

Just then the janitor, Mr. Mueller, went into the office. The janitor's kid was in the same class as my mom. He boldly said, "Let's call your mom one more time, and if she doesn't answer, then I will take you home in my truck." They called my grandma one more time, and sadly she didn't pick up. My mom tentatively went home in the janitor's truck.

When my mom finally got home, she ran to her mom, told her what had happened, and burst into tears. Mr. Mueller and my grandma exchanged their thank-yous, and the janitor departed.

After my mom stopped crying, her mom said, "You should write a story about this event, while I cook you some chicken and stars soup."

My mom did, and she drew a school bus on the front of the book, and titled it *The No Good Terrible Very Bad Day*. My mom still has that book to remind her that writing stories always makes her feel better.

Taylor Lim; Missouri, USA

Illustrator: Mya Gray; Missouri, USA

30.
Candy Thieves

1981; Olivette, Missouri, USA

My friend Josh and I were walking to a neighborhood candy store in Olivette, Missouri. It was 1981, and we were both in fifth grade. When we walked into the candy store, we realized we had no money. Josh told me we should just steal a candy bar while the store clerk wasn't looking. Josh whispered to me, "Don't let the clerk see you."

I took a chocolate bar off the shelf and tucked it into my back pocket while no one was watching. Then Josh carefully slid a candy bar up his sleeve. The clerk looked up just as the candy bar disappeared into Josh's sleeve. While Josh and I were heading toward the door, the clerk stepped in front of us and locked the door with an angry look on his face. We both knew at that moment we were in deep trouble.

"Empty your pockets now," the clerk ordered Josh.

There was nothing in Josh's pockets. The clerk reached out and touched Josh's sleeve and heard the crackling of the candy bar wrapper. I saw the store clerk reach for the store phone and dial 911. I felt fear rush over me, knowing the police would come and we would be arrested. While the store clerk was still on the phone, I took a few steps backwards. I pressed my back up to a food shelf. I carefully took out the candy bar from my back pocket and set it on the shelf. With the candy bar out of my back pocket, I felt so relieved.

A few minutes later, the neighborhood police officer rushed through the store door. I was scared to death! As we walked out of the candy shop, red and blue lights flashed in our eyes, and the noise of sirens filled the neighborhood with sound.

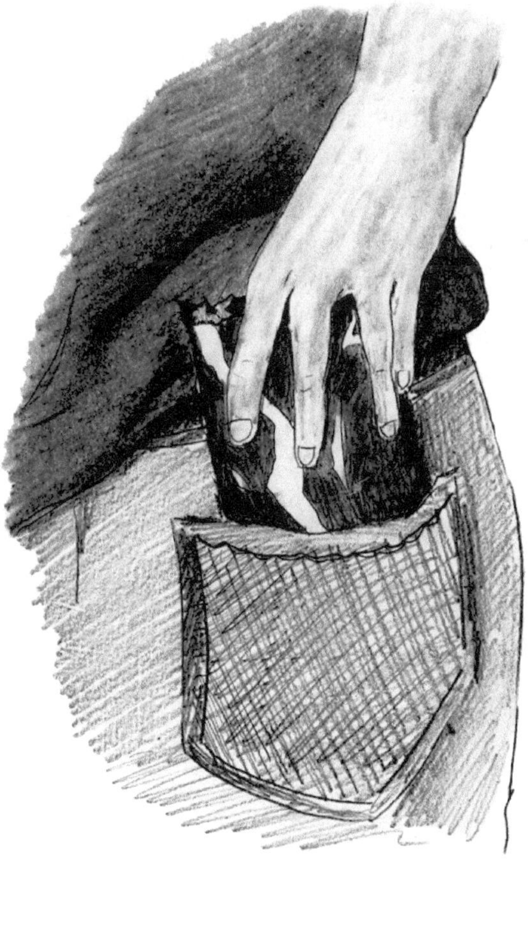

The policeman put us both in his police car. I sat in the back and didn't say a word. The policeman asked Josh a lot of questions, including "Where do you live?" "What's your name?" and "How old are you?" Josh answered all of the questions as he nervously rubbed his hands together. The officer didn't ask me any questions, because the clerk never saw me steal a candy bar.

Once the questions ended, we were driven to Josh's house. I stepped out of the car and followed Josh and the policeman.

"You can go home now, kid," he said to me, looking over his shoulder. I sprinted home, thinking about what just happened, feeling grateful I didn't get caught!

That day I learned to never steal anything in my entire life again.

Ella Munz, daughter of the narrator of the story; Missouri, USA

Illustrator: Janessa Hoffmann; Missouri, USA

31.
Grandfather, the Swimmer

1983; near Abadan, Khuzestan Province, Iran

It isn't until someone is faced with adversity that he or she begins to realize their full potential. The human body is capable of amazing feats when pushed to its limits. My grandfather knows this personally from his experience in 1983.

It was during the Iran-Iraq War, and my grandfather was part of the Iraqi Army. My grandfather was sent to capture Abadan, a city in Iran. The attack was a failure and many lost their lives, but luckily my grandfather made it.

After the attack, the Iranians chased the surviving Iraqis of the battalion back toward Iraq. The Iraqis were chased from midnight to noon. There was no time to rest. Being caught could result in torture or death! After being chased, they reached a river called "Shatt al-Arab."[1]

The Iranian Army chasing them was yet to arrive, as my grandfather and others were resting and contemplating on what to do next. Then they heard many footsteps. They looked around in confusion. Before my grandfather's battalion could find their bearings, they heard shouting, and shots began to be fired. They quickly realized it was the Iranians.

Many men were falling, and my grandfather realized his only hope was to swim across the river. The river was around 450 meters across (which is the same as swimming nine laps in an Olympic-size swimming pool). Although the distance wasn't that far, many people with assault rifles and bazookas were shooting at them. Swimming across the river would be an unbelievable feat to achieve.

Luckily for those who swam, there were small sandbars that would help them rest, but they could get shot if they rested. The Iranians continued chasing them on the shore to intercept them.

Much to Grandfather's dismay, he heard another Iraqi Army on the far side of the river. As he approached, he heard them berating those who ran, calling them "coward" and forcing them to return to battle. My grandfather recognized the group as Jaysh al Sha'bi. They had been stationed at this location to stop those who retreated from battle.

My grandfather was almost at the shore. He was close enough to hear Jaysh al Sha'bi yelling. The Iranian Army had caught up to both of the Iraqi battalions and started shooting at them. Even though Jaysh al Sha'bi's job was to stop soldiers from retreating, *they* ran away!

My grandfather and some of his friends found refuge in the reeds at the edge of the river. They slowly walked off, making sure not to make any noise, as they knew their lives depended on that. They marched until they reached a border post. That took most of the night. There they rested, regrouped, and lived to battle another day.

Ameer Jawad; Missouri, USA

1. Where this story takes place, Shatt al-Arab is the boundary between Iraq and Iran.

32.
The Note in the Cowbell

1985; St. Louis, Missouri, USA

Bob, as a junior high and high school football player, always had his mom cheering him on. He didn't play exciting positions. He played on the offensive line and as linebacker on defense. Sadly, he often found himself at the bottom of the piles, where everyone would jump onto each other at the end of every play. Now, Bob's mom realized it was hard to hear your mom cheering for you when you were at the bottom of the piles. She had to find a solution, but at the moment she couldn't find the right one.

In 1985 Bob was attending school at John Burroughs. The coach from the high school football team asked him if he wanted to join the team. Bob was ecstatic, because he was only a ninth grader, in junior high. His mom was also excited, since she loved football and especially loved watching her son play. However, his mom still wanted to find a way for him to hear her as she cheered him on.

A cowbell! That was it. Now from the bottom of the piles Bob would hear his mom shaking her cowbell like crazy and know she was there for him.

While attending Burroughs, Bob was blessed to be on a football team that made it to the state championship game. What an exciting time to play at Busch Stadium under the lights! This experience made Bob appreciate all the years that his mom had sacrificed everything to get him to practice every day, to wash his stinky uniforms, and to never miss a game. He had to do something to show his mom how appreciative he was of her.

On the night of the state championship game, the loudspeakers introduced Bob, and as he walked onto the field his mom shook the cowbell with all her strength. However, this time as she rang the bell, it didn't sound right. As she looked inside the cowbell, there was a note taped inside it that said, "This one's for you." Bob had left her a note expressing his appreciation for always being there for him. Her heart filled with warmth and pride.

That evening Burroughs claimed the title of 1985 Missouri 2A State Champion. The fans and players were screaming, cheering, and jumping up and down. While everyone else admired the state championship trophy, Bob's mom clutched her own cowbell trophy and whispered, "Thank you," to Bob.

Years later, when Bob had a wife and two children, his mom became ill and passed away. Bob helped his dad go through her belongings. While he was digging through the boxes, he found the cowbell with the note inside. Bob took this cowbell to his mom's funeral and rang it while whispering, "This one's for you."

Kate Bohlmann, Bob's daughter; Missouri, USA

33.
Where's the Cake?

1985; Winterville, North Carolina, USA

When members of a large family get together, funny things are going to happen. A funny thing happened one Thanksgiving at my great-grandma's house in Winterville, North Carolina. My mom was five years old. She and her siblings called this grandma "Mama Vera." She passed away when I was two years old, so I don't remember her at all. However, my mom said Mama Vera could make a great Thanksgiving feast.

For dessert that year Mama Vera had a beautiful coconut cake baked by a friend of hers. My mom says the cake cost twenty dollars, which was a lot of money for a cake in 1985. This cake was special, because it was made with fresh coconut, not with coconut from a can. The baker had to crack the coconut open, grate the fruit out, and save the juice. Each layer of the cake was soaked in coconut juice.

After everyone finished eating the delicious feast and dessert, all of the ladies spent an hour cleaning up. The stacks of china and silver had to be washed, dried, and put away for the next year. Then Mama Vera began looking for the coconut cake, because several people wanted another slice.

Everyone got up from the table and started looking for the cake, but no one could find the cake. Even Uncle Linwood, my great-great-uncle, started looking for the cake. Now he didn't actually get up to look for it. He just looked across the room from his seat and kept saying, "Where's the cake? Where's the cake?" Finally Uncle Linwood gave up on the others trying to find the cake. He slowly pulled himself up from the table to join the hunt.

That's when my mom spotted the cake. There it was in the chair, as flat as a pancake and twice as big around as before. Uncle Linwood had been sitting on the cake the whole time! He had fluffy white icing and coconut bits stuck to his pants. The funniest thing was he was still looking up and down for the cake. He just didn't look *behind* him! Everyone started chuckling, and by the time Uncle Linwood realized where the cake was, he was laughing, too.

Lucy Abbott Fader; North Carolina, USA

34.
The Chocolate Chip Cookies

c. 1989; Kinston, North Carolina, USA

My mom was always a responsible person and driver. She never got a speeding ticket, and was top of her class at Kinston High. One day while driving to Kinston High School, she got distracted by singing along to the radio. Since she was so distracted, she didn't notice how close she was getting to the mailboxes. As she edged closer and closer, suddenly — *BAM!* She hit someone's mailbox.

After realizing what she had done, she quickly exited the car to see the damage. The whole side mirror was off, and the mailbox was destroyed. My mom had no idea whose mailbox it was, but knew she must tell them what had happened. She walked up to the door as her heart was beating fast. She debated over and over whether she should ring that doorbell or just go to school and pretend that this had never happened.

Before she could make up her mind, an old lady opened the door. With one glance at the tears rolling down my mom's face and at her own wrecked mailbox, she understood exactly what had happened. My mom started to speak, but the lady cut her off and asked her if she would like to come in. My mom, unable to put any words together, simply nodded her head.

The old lady told her not to worry about the mailbox, because it was an accident. My mom had been babysitting all summer long, so she offered to repay the lady. The lady refused to let her do such a thing. She said that my mother would need all of that money for replacing the car's mirror. The lady also said that she had been looking for an excuse to get rid of that mailbox anyway. The old lady brought out the best chocolate chip cookies and tea that my mom has ever had. My mom said that she would never forget the smell of those chocolate chip cookies.

My mom had been so distraught about the mailbox that she had totally forgotten about school. She hopped into the car and drove to get the car fixed. The old lady was right about saving her money, for she had to give them all of her savings in order for them to fix her car.

The car was already fixed by the time school was over. No one could even tell that she'd had to get the mirror fixed. My grandparents never asked about the car and my mom never brought it up, but that doesn't mean that she will ever forget about that day or those chocolate chip cookies.

When my mom told me this story, I could not believe it. My perfect mom hit a mailbox. My mom always yells at my sister for driving recklessly, but my sister has never hit a mailbox. I love this story, because it is nice to know that not one person or object is perfect. But those cookies were pretty close.

Avery Johnson; North Carolina, USA

35.
Dine and Dash

c. 1991; North Highlands, California, USA

When my parents were dating in high school, they often switched off planning dates. My mother was a very creative person and decided to have a little bit more of a thrilling date when it was her turn to plan — more thrilling than my dad knew he was in for.

Once this date had entered my mom's mind, she knew there would be a lot of planning. See, my mom was planning for her and my dad to dine and dash — not literally, of course. As she started formulating the idea, she went to the owner of the restaurant they would be "stealing" from. She discussed with him what she was trying to do and how they would make sure beforehand that their meal would all be paid for. As soon as she got an okay from the owner, the plan could all fall into place.

The day came when my mom and dad were supposed to go on their date. My mom got ready, and she and my grandma went to pick up my dad. They got to the restaurant, and my grandma Jean dropped them off, with my mom purposely leaving her purse in the car. The waiters were in on the plan, too. They seated my parents far away from the door and somewhat near the restrooms. While my mom and dad were talking, my grandma Jean came in (posing as a customer) and was seated around the corner, where she would be unseen by my parents.

When they were ready for the check, the waiter took my mom the check, making sure to give it to her and not my dad. This was because the check didn't have anything on it. They had given the real check to my grandma around the corner, where she would pay for the meal for my parents. My dad didn't know this, of course. He didn't even know Grandma was in the building.

As my mother reached for her purse to pay, she acted surprised when she didn't have it. "Jared," my mother said, "I don't have my purse with me. I must have left it in the car. Can you pay?"

My father replied, "No, I don't have my wallet. I can't find it." The reason my dad couldn't find his wallet was that his mom had taken it from him to help the plan.

"Well, I guess we'll just have to dine 'n' dash," my mom replied. They formulated a plan to do such without being caught. My mom was to go into the bathroom, and when she returned she would just walk out the front door. A few minutes later my dad was supposed to do the same.

When they both had left successfully, they were going to call my grandma from the phone booth several minutes away from the restaurant. My dad heard a police siren in the distance and thought they had been caught. That's when my mom told my dad he had been pranked.

Cadence Andrus; Idaho, USA

Illustrators of *Volume 13*

7. Jasmine Flowers; Missouri, USA — "A Single Ring"
11. Cameron Churchich; Colorado, USA — "Kindness in Darkness"
15. Cecelia Vannoy; Missouri, USA — "Importance of Rainwater"
17. Yuka Iwasawa; Missouri, USA — "A Wrong Turn"
18. Devyn Shelton; Missouri, USA — "Pocket Alarm"
19. Janessa Hoffmann; Missouri, USA — "Sammy's Rough Road Trip"
23. Miles Montgomery O'Dwyer; Missouri, USA — "Hard Work Down the Drain (Almost)"
24. Janessa Hoffmann; Missouri, USA — "SOS — Saving Our Sand Dune" (Also on cover)
27. Lawson Holestine; Missouri USA — "How a Bull Taught Me How to Shave"
28. Walker Brand; Missouri, USA — "The Tornado"
29. Mya Gray; Missouri, USA — "The No Good Terrible Very Bad Day"
30. Janessa Hoffmann; Missouri, USA — "Candy Thieves"

Invitation to Participate

The Grannie Annie Family Story Celebration invites you to discover, write, and submit a story from your family's history. Your story can be humorous, tragic, inspirational — it can be about *anything* that happened in your family before you were born. The annual submission deadline is February 1. Complete details, including the guidelines and required submission form, are available on The Grannie Annie's website.

Grannie Annie Storykeepers 2018 and Their Story Titles

Tzipporah Abrahamson — "A Concert to Remember"

Avital Abramova — "My Grandmother Sells Ice Cream"

Hailey Jo Adams — "Bed Check Charlie"

Esther Akilov — "The Accident at the Carousel"

Mallory Allen — "The Treehouse"

Saraa Alsharif — "Trade and Family Success"

Avigail Aminov — "Tough Life for Grandpa"

D'Naija Ammons — "The Firework Incident"

Cadence Andrus — "Dine and Dash"

Channa Asher — "A Soldier's Kindness"

Tsofia T. Atlas — "Telling Another Hagaddah"

Rebecca Avila — "The Shoe That Flew"

Hannah Azose — "The Stowaway"

Chaya Baalhaness — "Flowers in Philadelphia"

Rebecca Bailey — "Inspirational Cancer"

Beno Ballard — "The Basketball Game"

Nathan Barasch — "Military Dad"

Logan Barnswell — "Horse and Dog Biscuits"

Jack Barwick — "The Portrait That Was Meant to Be Found"

Elizabeth Bauer — "The Misplaced Meeting"

Reagan Beachy — "The Stick"

Brody Bean — "The Big Game"

Andrew Bedmer — "Uncle John's Balloon Bag"

Olivia Begelman — "A Trip to the Store"

Amelia Bendick — "Australian War Bride"

Sammi Bergjans — "Wogs' Revenge"

Carter Bergkoetter — "The Splash That Hurt"

Becca Berkmeyer — "Uncle Bob's #1 Fan"

Julia Bernal — "The Paint Incident"

Nicole Bernal — "The Lost Day"

Leah Berutti — "The Safe"

Noah Beyer — "Graveyard Scare"

Ava Biermann — "The City Bus"

Vince Bischof — "The Life of Glenn Bischof"

Ava Blair — "Camping Shenanigans"

Grace Blair — "Broken Neck"

Emma Bland — "A True Love Story"

Rochel Blumberg — "The Escape"

Tara Bobo — "Wallace in the Courthouse"

Kate Bohlmann — "The Note in the Cowbell"

Lilly G. Boschert — "A Fishy Situation"

Brock Bowman — "Importance of Rainwater"

Christopher Lawrence Braggs — "The Unexpected Occasion"

Alex Brand — "Nathan and the Torah Scrolls"

Sofia Brantley — "The Midnight Reckoning"

Eliana Braun — "How Brave Could You Be?"

Nick Brengarth — "The Long Journey"

Tori Brennan — "The Day Our Babysitter Quit"

Gershon Brill — "The Passover Bug!"

Evey Bringolf — "Water Skiing Catastrophe"

Melayna Brown — "Grandpa Hook"

Jake Browning — "Transferred on 9/11"

Isabella Buckley — "Grandma's Dog and the Stinky Skunk"

Lola Burt — "The Runaway Ring"

Mia Butcher — "A New Way to Hay"

Jaxon Campbell — "Aftermath of the Navy"
Cooper Capdeboscq — "Snow Days"
Kendra Cargill — "Champ"
Aidan Carney — "The Morning Surprise"
Brooke Carter — "Tricycle Runaway"
Lilly Charnes — "The Chicken Coop Catastrophe"
Elnatan Chasser — "My Cousin, the Baker"
Mary Neal Cheek — "Two Friends Meet Up After Thirty Years!"
Jack Chelew — "The Amazing Horse"
Anica Cherian — "The Trip"
Inaya Chishti — "A Midnight Meeting"
Lucy Christian — "Big Banana"
Elanor Churchill — "The Forgotten Sister"
Elizabeth Clawson — "A Wrong Turn"
Lily Cofer — "Two Weddings for One Couple"
William Collings — "The Winter Struggle"
Tyler Collison — "First Memory at a New Home"
Mary Isabel Concagh — "The Muddy Shoe"
Lexi Connolly — "The Super-Duper Looper"
Parker Corey — "Was It Worth It?"
Colin Cornett — "How the Course of History Changed"
Henry Counts — "The Eventful Move"
Drew Cox — "The Farmer and the Mule"
Zachary Creek — "Wingman in Trouble"
Lizzy Crowe — "King of Hamilton Street"
Ellie Curran — "I Think I'll Keep My Glasses"
Jack Dacey — "Green Lake"
Ruth Davidov — "Growing Up Alone"
Yael Davidov — "Surviving the War with a Miracle"

Brysan Davis — "The Proposal"

Riley Dean — "Kicked Out of the House"

William DeBoer — "Eggs"

Tess Degenhart — "Grandma's Dollar"

Allison DeLassus — "The Tale of the Short Tail"

Alex DeLuna — "BMX Nun"

Elana DeRiso — "The Rattlesnake"

Bex Derr — "All Aboard"

Leah Deutscher — "Between Life and Death"

Dassi Dick — "The Escape"

Rylan Dickens — "Outlaw Uncle"

Ethan Dixon — "Leather Bullwhips, Chiclets, and Wooden Spinning Tops"

Addie Draper — "Sandra's Adventure"

Isabel Draper — "Sammy's Rough Road Trip"

Chance Duncan — "Crossing the Line"

Lucas Eardley — "The Gun Accident"

Alex Ebling — "A Snowy Tradition"

Rebecca Ehrenhaus — "The Crazy Cruise to Alaska"

Shoshana Eisner — "Name Trouble"

Ava Elias — "Refugees"

Reagan Engel — "The Helicopter Chase"

Mordechai Engelsohn — "The Helper"

Phoebe Epstein — "The Man at the Gas Station"

Maggie Erker — "My Brother's Adventurous Day"

Bailee Erlbaum — "The Sabbath Crisis"

Isabella Carolina Figeroa España — "A Long Walk"

Anayeli Herrera Espinoza — "Is It True Love?"

John Evans — "A Loyal Friend"

Lily Evans — "The Upturned Carpet"

Sam Evans — "A Shoe Problem"
Lydia Fabian — "The Cow Run"
Lucy Abbott Fader — "Where's the Cake?"
Nicholas Faguett — "Haunted"
Emma Fairchild — "A Bad Crash"
Virginia Fanning — "Bumpy Backseat Birth"
Michal Feder — "The Pocket Watch"
Raul Firnhaber — "My Dad's Journey to America"
Leah Fischer — "A Whole New World"
Jacob Fisher — "Betty"
Maegan Fleming — "The Crazy Prank"
Rosa Forget — "The Way of Water"
Nathan Fox — "The Zigmaw"
Shira Frank — "Danger! Danger!"
Joshie Frankel — "Escaping the Holocaust"
Bailey Grace Franklin — "All About That Money"
Caroline N. Franklin — "Shrimp in My Pocket"
William Boyd French — "Orange Juice?"
Abby Freund — "Farm Life Ain't Easy"
Hadassa Friedman — "Saved"
Shifra Froehlich — "Double Kindness"
Megan Fuller — "The Snake and the Frog"
Claire Fulton — "Not So Super Mike"
Tzipora Fuzailov — "Miracles"
Daksh Gahlot — "A Widow's Story"
Matan Galanti — "Student Struggle for Soviet Jewry"
Bella Gambaro — "Gretchen's Three-Year-Old Chef"
Shaindy Ganz — "A Very Special Person"
Heidi Gardner — "Cousin, Beware!"

Delia Gates — "The Snowmen"

Shira Gavrielov — "The Lost Snake"

James Ryan Geary — "The Glass Submarine"

Garrett Gilgo — "The Big Yank"

Madeline Gill — "Never a Winner in War"

Tyler Gillispie — "Grandpa Goes to Heaven"

Drew Gingerich — "A Horrible Mess"

Sanaa Glasper — "The Elevator Shaft"

Leah Glatt — "Under the Table"

Noa Goldschmidt — "Science Project Gone Wrong"

Allison Goldstein — "The Christmas Eve Tradition"

Azi Goldstein — "The Dirt Mouth"

Erika Gorrin-Rivas — "Their Lives in Two Suitcases"

Ever Grae — "Is the Tree Stable?"

Willa Grawer — "Throwing Away Toys"

Alyssa Greco — "The Great Escape"

Olivia Green — "Life on a Farm"

Devorah Greenberg — "One Letter Saves a Life"

Avigayil Greenfeld — "Not on Saturday"

Olivia Greenlee — "Dr. Evil's Dog"

Chava B. Greenstein — "Dybbuk Removal"

Kruesi Griffin — "An Experience to Remember"

Abigale V. Grubb — "A Painful 4th of July"

Leya Gruenbaum — "Coming to America"

Ilonka Guilliams — "The Backyard Coaster"

Banks Gurganus — "The Pistol"

Ben Gustafson — "The Proposal"

Anna Haddad — "I've Got a Sweet Tooth for You"

Everette Haddad — "The Apple and the Parsley"

Lauren Hagedorn — "Rows of Learning"
Tamar Haim — "The Adventures of My Grandmother"
Zachary M. Haironson — "Nathan Lerman, the Jewish Rudy!"
Crawford Hall — "The Scariest Accident"
Seth Hardee — "Pork Rinds"
Rosa Hargrove — "The Crash"
Aliza Harpaz — "My Special Aunt Eynat"
Kate Harper — "A Perilous Journey"
Noa Temima Harris — "Can't I Go to School?"
Savannah Harrison — "A Father to the Fatherless"
Will Hartman — "Trouble in Math Class"
Samuel Hearon-Isler — "God's House"
Taylor Heimbaugh — "A Family's Commitment to Service"
Hannah Henderson — "Moving to America"
Addie Henke — "Hardships for the Henrys"
Sam Herrera — "A Strange Tragedy?"
Ava Herschberg — "The Goose"
Malka Herskowitz — "The Unlikely Match"
Ashley Hill — "Wedding Mishaps"
Savannah Hines — "Kids in Need"
Grace Hirtz — "Bringing Baby Jeff Home"
Nastia Hnatov — "Cavity Car"
Lizzie Hogan — "Surviving Pearl Harbor"
Hayden M. Holesko — "Don't Give Up in the Desert"
Beau Holmes — "My Mom's Mischievous Adventures"
Hannah Hood — "Living in Critical Conditions"
Mary Helen Hood — "Surprise Trip to Cuba"
Ava Hornburg — "My Mom and the Monkey"
Malkie Horowitz — "The Family That Grew and Grew and Grew"

Tyler Hott — "A Tough Decision"
Caroline Jennie Howard — "Gun-to-the-Head Bank Robbery"
Cole Howard — "What Should We Name Him?"
Sydney Howard — "The Grandmother of a Century"
Marin Hugge — "*Ça commence à travers un océan*"
Miles Sorenson Hulka — "A Dinner of Pearls"
Kyle Hunt — "Trip Across America"
Wade Hunter — "The Soccer Career"
Meimona S. Ibrahim — "Girls, Not Brides"
William Iott — "Dad vs. Train"
Abby Irwin — "The Big Snowstorm!"
Anna Irwin — "Saved from Criminals"
Naomi Irwin — "Maryellen and the Celebration"
Jerome Iskander — "Lost in the City"
Avigail Israeli — "My Father's Incredible Escape"
Leora Itshakov — "Every Baby Counts"
Atara Jacobs — "The Story of Lola and Baruch"
Alaina Jakutowicz — "The Squirrel with the V-Shaped Tail"
Ameer Jawad — "Grandfather, the Swimmer"
Aneesha Rani Jayaram — "Falling into the Well"
Arjun S. Jayaraman — "Stuck in an Avalanche"
Taniya Jessie — "The Indestructible Shoes"
Alexis A. Johnson — "Trip to the E.R."
Ava C. Johnson — "The Worst Storm Ever"
Avery Johnson — "The Chocolate Chip Cookies"
Jaden Johnson — "Pocket Alarm"
Aaron Jones — "My Uncle, the Purple Heart Recipient"
Cameron Jones — "The Most Thankful Thanksgiving"
Gracee Jones — "The Last Draft of Vietnam"

Evan Jordan — "The Cement Hole"
Miriam Jungreis — "Surviving the Holocaust"
Elizabeth Kadyk — "The Long Journey of Charles Lear Sadler"
Tehilla Kaffash — "Fierce and Strong"
Malka Kalati — "The Spooky Lady"
Delaney Kaman — "Separated By the Sea"
Keren Kazakov — "The Train"
Drew Kearney — "Clinton Charles Barnes"
Landon Kearney — "The Trap"
Molly Kell — "The Purple Heart"
Batsheva Keller — "Shoveling the Snow"
Connor Kendrick — "Brain Cancer"
Hannah Kendrick — "Pocket Rocket"
Jackson Kent — "Almost Dead"
Rami Kessock — "To Live"
Aliyah Khalil — "The Fate of Daffy, the Duck"
Micah Khalil — "The Race Through Death Valley"
Leah Khiyayev — "Sewing a Friendship"
Nyah Kim — "The Name"
Emma Kinard — "My Family's History"
Yoni Klein — "My Grandparents' Story"
Benjamin Klinger — "Shmuel—Brooklyn, NY, NY"
Shalva Rachel Kobre — "Glass Can Pierce Your Heart"
Chris Koener — "The Well-Known Riot"
Daniella Kohan — "A Life to Take Care"
Tzipora Korn — "The Great Baby Surprise"
Carmen J. Kosmicki — "Hairy Eggs"
Devorah Kramer — "Ten Is Too Old"
Kendal Kraner — "The Great Race Surprise"

Etai Kreitner — "Eda's Amazing Adventure with Life"
Henry Krey — "Chiptastrophe"
Ella Kuhlman — "The Terror of 9/11"
Madelynn Kuhn — "The Great Flood"
Rochel Kurz — "My *Great* Great-Grandmother"
Holly Kwapiszeski — "Safari Adventure Gone Terribly Wrong"
Bree LaFevers — "How My Family Got Banished from England"
Jordan LaGrone — "The Almost Terrible Accident"
Tyler Laskowski — "Grandpa's Fishing Trip"
Adalie Lauth — "Divorce Problems"
Malka Lavner — "Kindness in Darkness"
Alexis Laws — "Home Alone"
Tien Le — "Hard Work Down the Drain (Almost)"
Zachary Leeker — "Thomas and the Train"
Eva Lemon — "The Snail Incident"
Ethan Lenefsky — "The Science Project and the Mice"
Caleb Leonard — "Grandpa's Story"
Shani Levy — "The Embarrassing Event"
Claire Lewis — "Lucky on the *Lusitania*"
Haynes Lewis — "The Man Who Lost Everything"
Garrett Liberman — "The Blind Lifeguard"
Caden Lieberman — "Cheer Team"
Jonathan Lieberman — "Run for Your Life"
Anna Grace Likes — "Spaghetti-Oh-No"
Taylor Lim — "The No Good Terrible Very Bad Day"
Taylor Llewellyn — "Dilemma in Daytona"
Asher Lowry — "Making Football History"
Evan Luke — "The Rail Ride"
Maria Luna — "St. Therese Novena"

Adina Irene Lustig — "The Lost Train to Bruges"
Allie Lytle — "The Great Escape"
Jimmy MacDonald — "The Trip"
Chana Esther Machlis — "The Real Diamond"
Keira Makalintal — "My Great-Grandfather's Legacy"
Kaitlyn S. Mann — "The Joyride"
Rina Marcus — "Who's On Board?"
Emily Mark — "A Single Ring"
Lucy Marsh — "Hunting for Moses"
Caden Martens — "My Great-Grandfather"
Julia Martin — "The Day My Grandma Learned to Pick Up Her Toys"
Olivia Martinez — "The Spirit Bridge"
Isaac Maryles — "World Series"
Sophie Maupin — "The Big Scare"
Abigail McClune — "Single Bullet"
Maya McConnell — "Backpacking Through Europe"
Aidan McCoy — "Bloody Hill"
Connor McCoy — "A Hero on Thin Ice"
Margaret McDaniel — "Grandma's Beginnings"
Mason McElveen — "Birthday and the Snake"
Ava Grace McGowan — "'Building' a Better Life"
Max McGuire — "Fifth Grade in Japan"
George McGuire-Murillo — "Grandma's Christmas Confession"
Owen McMurtrie — "All Because of a Kilt, Eh?"
Morgan McPhaul — "The Mitigating Waters of Shatley Springs"
Hodaya Meir — "A Surprising Letter"
Odel Meirov — "The Coolest Things About My Grandmother and My Mother"
Max Mentel — "Scared of Nothing"
Arden Menzel — "The Trip"

Makayla Brown Messex — "Children of the Corn"
Braiden Metzger — "Weekend Vacation"
Ahren Meuhleisen — "The Underage Welders"
Abigail Meyer — "I Was Forced To"
Emma Miller — "The Flying Messengers of World War II"
Quinn Miller — "The Indian and Dear Ma"
Yael Miller — "Scary Snowy Sunday"
Carissa Mitchell — "A Beastly Encounter"
Luke Moeller — "The Missed Opportunity"
Emma Mohler — "The Roof Mishap"
Ally Molitor — "My Papa's Life in the Orphanage"
Aspen Monning — "The Goose"
Riley Moore — "Girl on the Go"
Lauren E. Morris — "The Best Christmas Ever"
Nell Mason Morris — "The Woman Who Caught on Fire"
Avery Morrow — "Protesting"
Aliza Moskowitz — "Hiding in the Woods"
Elia Movahed — "The Chocolae Thieves"
Makky Mozie — "From Grass to Grace"
Jadyn Mueller — "Davie's Rock"
Stephanie Muigai — "Ten Thousand Miles from Home"
Will Mullen — "The Conagra Feed Plant Explosion"
Ella Munz — "Candy Thieves"
Michal Chaya Muradov — "The Tragedy of the Twin Towers"
Naomi Muratov — "Rock in a Pot"
Sean James Murphy, Jr. — "The Greatest Adventure"
Dace Murray — "Ella Ray Hankins Murray Burr"
Carolann Muschick — "A Holiday Surprise"
Daliya Mushiyev — "The Great Saver"

Josie Naeger — "Sneaky Kittens"
Mayu Nakano — "Friends and Enemies (Japan)"
Chava Nat — "The Show That Must Go On"
Lily Naylor — "Friends and Enemies (United States)"
Dierks Nekoliczak — "The Snowy Wedding"
Thomas Newhall — "Changing a Life"
Alex Newman — "A Personal Situation"
Elisheva Niazov — "Exempt from War"
Anna Niekamp — "The Naked Geese"
Lindie Nielsen — "Mysterious Cat"
Madeline Furn Nogar — "Lost at Sea"
Shira Nordlicht — "The Mysterious Man"
Rachel Norris — "Lost for a Taste of Home"
Jamie Obertop — "The Driving Adventure"
Lainey Ojeda — "Butterflies in My Stomach"
Victor Ojeda — "Angry Bugs"
Lulu Olszweski — "The Miracle Child"
Amelia Opphile — "Journey to a New World"
Natalie Ori — "Childhood"
Holden Orrick — "Alone"
Ella Ortbals — "The Fight"
Christian Ouano — "May 21, 1943: Bomber Down"
Raizy Pacht — "On the Way to New York"
Bella Pagano — "Love at First Sight"
Mary Grace Paige — "Arrowhead Bandit"
Maya Parafiniuk — "Living in Communism"
Henri Paris — "Henri de Marcellus"
Kenneth Patrick III — "The Battery Contest"
Tommy Paul — "Faultless Oil Company"

Kaden A. Peer — "Once a Tar Heel, Always a Tar Heel"
Jack Maurice Pendleton — "You Never Know"
Ryan Pense — "Injured in Training"
Chedva Perlman — "The Worst Doll"
Jordan Perry — "Five-Year-Old Lifesaver"
Ely Perry IV — "Mako Shark Attack"
Leora Peyser — "The Showers"
Hindy Pfeiffer — "Twin!"
Anna Piasecki — "Running from the Cow"
Anagi Pieris — "The Lunar Rock Legacy"
Rikki Plawes — "Getting a Visa"
Brooks Plumb — "Growing Up in Topsail Beach"
Kylie Plumb — "My Ship Has Sailed"
Annika Pollack — "On the Ropes"
Natalie Poss — "Hot Dog"
Anthony Puetz — "Ted's Mountain Adventure"
Aliza Putney — "A Night at the Train Station"
Benny J. Quéré — "The Long Immigration to America"
Gabriel Radabaugh — "The Biggest Tree"
Matthew Radford — "The Death of My Granddad"
Yael Rafailov — "The Scary Adventure"
Caroline Rahal — "The Mishap"
Cal Ramthun — "Water Hero"
Eric Reed — "The Chandelier"
Owen Reinsch — "The Worst Pet Ever"
Chavy Reiss — "The Man in Stripes"
Helen Remington — "The Train from Fort Wayne"
Sam Rhodes — "Helen's Disastrous Pig Chase"
Lauren Elizabeth Richardson — "Lost in Her Dream"

Wyatt Roberts — "The Dresden Nobody Knows About"
Kayla Robertson — "The Great UFO"
Kylie Robertson — "The Fantastic Fan Fail"
Kate McKinley Robinson — "An Accidental Love Story"
Grace Rogerson — "My Soldier, My Hero"
Samantha Roggenkamp — "The Marmalade Mistake"
Jack Roppa — "Blanc Blanc"
Eden Rosenstock — "Evacuate"
Mack Rosenstock — "The Stowaway's Escape"
Chaya Rosenthal — "The War Against the British"
Talya Rosman — "Her Prized Possession"
Madison Rosner — "A Survival Story"
Jenaye Ross — "Watch Your Mouth!"
Sugulah Chaya Rubinov — "Keeping the Sabbath"
Landen Sackett — "The Bull Chase"
Logan Sackett — "The Van"
Caleb Sanderson — "My Mom"
Faiga Savetsky — "Pesach"
Grant Sawyer — "The Unlikely Adventure"
Ahuva Esther Schechter — "Grandpa Kleg and the Ku Klux Clan"
Andrew Schiltz — "The Perfect Watermelon"
Sara Schloss — "Suffocating Church Service"
Sabrina Schultz — "The Attack"
Alex Schwartz — "Escape to the New World"
Mattea Schwartz — "Annapurna"
Lauren Grace Segrave — "Birds, Planes, and Fire"
Shirel Shaool — "All Because of the Steps"
Goldie Shapiro — "When My Grandfather Got Arrested"
Vivyann Shearer — "Red"

Alex Shelton — "The Orange Bowl Nightmare"
Piper Shepard — "Help"
Sean Shepard — "Historical James Bond"
Terran Shepard — "A 5,000-Mile Journey"
Mary L. Sheppard — "The D.A.R.E. Program"
Tim Shoemaker — "Broken Down"
Yafa Shriki — "My Great-Grandpa Max"
Daniel Shulman — "David Cone's Perfect Game"
Abbey Siburt — "The Worst Trip to the Grocery Store Ever"
Abigail Siess — "Leaving Home"
Chana Simhaee — "The Journey"
Audrey Sims — "Once in a Lifetime"
Diya Singh — "In Sickness and in Health"
Ivy Slen — "Let Us Not Forget"
Taylor Grace Sliva — "The Gargantuan Hole to China"
Ward Sloan — "Daisy"
Ronan Smith — "Trip to Bali, Indonesia"
Lance Smithwick — "A Man, a Gun, and a Granddad"
Noam Smus — "Holy Cow"
Chani Soffer — "Generations"
Shellye Solomon — "The Brothers Are Late for School"
Marissa Solverud — "The Accident in Germany"
Oscar Sorkin — "Worth the Wait"
Lauren E. Sowers — "Big Poop"
Zahava Speiser — "The North Star"
Mary Kate Spellman — "Sweet Sisters"
Mae St. John — "The Strength of Faith and Patience"
Avery Stanfill — "The Battle of the Coral Sea"
Erin Steinberg — "A Kind of Unusual Love Story"

Hadassa Steinberg — "The Richest Man's Microwave"
Brooke Stigall — "Away from Family"
Sarah Stockton — "Jail Shock"
Treyven Straka — "The Big Hunt"
Gregory G. Strauss — "The Secret Love for a Fluffy Turtle"
Katie Stuckel — "The Holy Rosary"
Skylar Andrew Studdard — "Hostage"
Dov Stulberger — "World Trade Center"
Thomas Stump — "The Three-Legged Reindeer"
Brody Sutto — "High School Athletics"
Yaffa Tabibov — "Laundry"
Chana Leah Taib — "Don't Mess with My Grandmother"
JoJo Talit — "Do You Believe in Miracles?"
Lily Tannenbaum — "Pig Chase"
Arieana Tatkenhorst — "Potato Soup Serial Killer"
Hudson Taylor — "The Fire Rampage"
Rina Tchatchanachvili — "Trust"
Shifra Tendler — "The Chicken March"
Madison Thigpen — "Ski Trip Gone Wrong"
Hannah Thom — "A Day at the Lake Gone Bad"
Gia Thomas — "Rolling Through the Night"
Jake Thomas — "The Rat Robbery"
Elizabeth Thuro — "The Baking Disaster"
Laney Torbit — "A Pilot with a Nosebleed"
Isabella Toschlog — "The Search in the Rain"
A. W. Tribula — "Three Unknown"
Shaindy Tropper — "A Great Rabbi's Blessing"
Shelby Truitt — "The Cub Scout and the Snake"
James Unwin — "Blizzard Mansion"

Dominik Usery — "The Big River Bushwhacker"
Charlotte Vannoy — "The Adoption"
Grace Vasher — "The Hanging Gardens of Disaster"
Ziv Yedidia Vayner — "The War"
Ashley Vieluf — "Love at First Checkout"
Isabella Vlaytchev — "The Loss of a Friend"
Brynley Wall — "USS *Forrestal*"
Carolista Walsh — "SOS — Saving Our Sand Dune"
Elsa Whitney Sawyer Walz — "How a Bull Taught Me How to Shave"
Sarala Weiner — "A Passover to Remember!"
Adel Weinman — "The Journey That Led to Victory"
Sophia Weiss — "Torn-ado"
B. J. Wesley — "The Contest"
Kathryn Wessels — "The Slippery Ice Pond"
Libby Wessels — "On the Move"
Livy West — "Broken Down"
Reese Westhoff — "The Day That Changed My Life"
Brynn Whitley — "The Fire of '94"
Rachel Wieder — "The New York City Blackout of 1977"
Ethan Wienstroer — "The Tornado"
Ben Wiley — "Teeth"
Jordan Williams — "Couch Down"
Kobi Williams — "Scissors Man!"
Mackenzie Williams — "What Homework?"
Jacob Winkelmann — "A Walking Miracle"
Drew Winkler — "John's Hard Life"
Emma-Kate Winter — "There's Always Something Else"
Miriam Wischnitzer — "Indian Matzah"
Annie Wood — "An Expensive Accident"

Olivia Wright — "Oops, That's Not the Brake"

Courtney Wu — "My Mom's Journey to America"

Emma Wyeth — "If Only Cell Phones Existed"

Bracha-Mazal Yagudayev — "The Melted Pan"

Ariella Yakubov — "The Impossible Was Done"

Miriam Yafa Yusupov — "The Unhappy Party"

Avital Yusupova — "The Journey of Keeping Shabbos"

Rivka Zacaim — "The Surprise War"

Jonah T. Zell — "Our One-Eared Baby"

Praise for The Grannie Annie

Thanks for such a great opportunity to write powerful stories and to showcase our work!

—Carol Fitzsimmons, Teacher; Missouri, USA

The Grannie Annie has brought all 51 children in my language arts classes closer to their families — and to each other. When they discuss their stories, they notice similarities between their own stories and their classmates' stories. The Grannie Annie is a valuable program that has provided my students and me with a powerful learning opportunity.

—Elie Bashevkin, Teacher; New York, USA

The Grannie Annie gives students and their parents a chance to reflect on the varied experiences that weave together their family's identity. Many people have brokenness in their family history, and by identifying and writing about hard experiences, our children learn to see the strength and restoration of our loved ones. We're grateful to The Grannie Annie for providing an opportunity to publicly show honor and respect to our family members who have persevered.

—Christan Perona, Parent; Missouri, USA

Participating in The Grannie Annie offers my students a wonderful opportunity to learn about their families' history by interviewing a family member, and an authentic audience for their writing.

—Kathy Lewis, Teacher; Missouri, USA

Perhaps the greatest value of the Grannie Annie stories is something not written in the book. When a child interviews an older relative, the child gets to know a person he or she may have taken for granted. The relative gets to tell a story that might have been lost. A bond is created or strengthened. A story is recorded for posterity. New memories are woven, and — just maybe — a writer is born.

—Lulu Delacre, Author/illustrator of *Salsa Stories*

My daughter, Sophia Rose, contacted my mother in Germany after her language arts teacher suggested that she write a story about my mother in World War II. The two had a wonderful e-mail and phone correspondence over a couple of weeks. When I saw the final draft of my daughter's writing, I read a story my mother had never told me. My daughter created a new memory of my mother's life through her writing. What an amazing gift The Grannie Annie gave our family!

—Petra Swidler, Parent; Missouri, USA

Because of The Grannie Annie, I have been motivated to continue writing and am now working on my first novel!

—Aaron Schnoor, Author, *Grannie Annie, Vols. 5, 6,* and *7*; Grannie Annie Selection Committee 2014, 2015, 2016, and 2017; North Carolina, USA

This is my daughter's first time submitting her writing outside her school. It's very encouraging to her. She loves reading and writing. I believe this experience will have a great impact on her.

—Daniel Liu, Parent; New Jersey, USA

When young people participate in The Grannie Annie and discover, and then reflect upon, their family's stories and the family stories of others, the experience can create in each of these young authors an enhanced sense of appreciation, understanding, and "connection." Thank you to The Grannie Annie for giving our communities young people who will see our diversity as an asset rather than a deficit, will recognize the sameness even in our differences, and will bring to our world a bit more compassion.

—Dr. Phil Hunsberger, Senior Partner, Educational Equity Consultants

Year after year, my fifth-grade students are eager and excited to submit their work to The Grannie Annie. The experience of submitting a manuscript — with the hope of publishing — gives newfound meaning to their learning. The students stand taller when they become cognizant that the world is benefiting from their contribution.

—Rebecca Friedman, Teacher; Maryland, USA

When I showed my student his illustration in the book, the whole class gave him an ovation. Thanks so very much for providing him with this opportunity to succeed.

—Clayvon Wesley, Teacher; Missouri, USA

Thank you for starting such a heartwarming project where *all* the kids are winners, whether their stories are published or not.

—G-g Metzger, Teacher; Texas, USA

Publication of our daughter's story is special to us for so many reasons. . . . Both my mother and grandmother passed away a few years ago. Growing up, I heard this story countless times from my grandmother. It's wonderful seeing that story told through my daughter's words.

—Andrea Rominger, Parent; Alabama, USA

The Grannie Annie provides the perfect opportunity for students to start asking questions about their families' past — not just the facts, but the stories. Then as they write, students begin to understand how *telling a story* differs from *writing a biography of facts*.

—Mark Futrell, Teacher; North Carolina, USA

Orion's writing a family story was extremely important to his grandmother, who had a serious illness. When he called her to tell her that his story was going to be published, she was as happy as anyone had seen her in months. She read the story to anyone who would listen. I can't even begin to tell you the positive impact that this has had on our family.

—Andrew Jones, Parent; Pennsylvania, USA

I would like to thank you for giving Yifu such an encouragement, and working diligently to publish his first article! Our families in China are very happy to hear about this. It is an amazing experience to me that I witness that a part of my family heritage is being connected from my father to my son through the event you support! Thank you!

—Yuxing Feng, Parent; Missouri, USA

This book should be on the bookshelves in all elementary and junior high schools.

—The Reading Tub™, www.TheReadingTub.com

My students were so excited to write their family stories! Since the stories were written during our immigration unit, the students had even more reason to ask their families questions. The stories really enriched our classroom discussions and helped the students to connect to the concepts being taught.

—Amy Del Coro, Teacher; New Jersey, USA

Since my mother died recently, I have been cleaning out her house and going through her things and wondering, "Who made this quilt? Who's in this old photo?" Trying to remember the family stories that she told me has really driven home the need to preserve family history. It is so wonderful that The Grannie Annie encourages this continuity of memories.

—Beverly Miller, Teacher; Alabama, USA

The Grannie Annie is a good start for kids to get published. And I love the way The Grannie Annie helps people understand their family history. It also helps children get closer to their families.

—Andrew Malphurs, Author of the *Grannie Annie, Vol. 5,* story "Grandpa's Saddle"; Georgia, USA

The Grannie Annie challenged my students to go beyond their comfort zone, to write for a broader audience, and to see that learning goes beyond the four walls of a classroom.

—Ann-Marie Harris, Teacher; Maryland, USA

Since first becoming involved with The Grannie Annie, we look forward every year to the truly unique and heartwarming stories each student brings to the classroom.

—Brian Billings and Laura Amburgey, Teachers; Ohio, USA

Stories connect people in families and communities, giving them a common language and understanding of the present as well as the past. Through The Grannie Annie, generations connect as students take time to listen to the stories of their older relatives — and learn from them. Then, as the students write and share their stories, the connections multiply.

—Amy Glaser Gage; Children's author, writing teacher, and consultant to The Grannie Annie

Although most students in our Eastern European village live next door to family members from earlier generations, The Grannie Annie prompted them to talk with their grandparents in new ways — and to discover the customs and challenges of times past. In addition, stories from the Grannie Annie books have given my students a glimpse of the world outside their village, where differences may abound but the underlying human condition remains the same.

—Martin Ellinger-Locke, Peace Corps volunteer in Glodeni, Moldova

The Grannie Annie is remarkable in its goals and in its approach. Recording and sharing the stories of preceding generations goes to the heart of education — it teaches us who we are as family members, citizens, and members of human civilization.

—Matthew Lary, Co-author of *Victory Through Valor: A Collection of World War II Memoirs*

The Grannie Annie is all about connection. As it hearkens back to the original Grannie Annie, it continues her tradition of oral storytelling to link generations and cultures. Grannie Annie family stories written by young people illuminate a long span of history, often revealing family values honed from adversity or triumph and tempered by humor and love.

—Janet Grace Riehl, Author of *Sightlines: A Family Love Story in Poetry & Music*

Our son's *oma* is overwhelmed that her "story" is in print in *Grannie Annie*. . . . Every family member and family friend has a signed copy.

—Karie Millard, Parent; Indiana, USA

My son "harvested" several stories from my father, including one that appeared in *Grannie Annie, Vol. 1*. My father has since passed away, and I am forever grateful that my son recorded these stories before it was too late. I doubt he would have done so if it had not been for The Grannie Annie.

—Karen Metcalf, Parent; Tennessee, USA

When kids learn details about what life was like decades ago, the past comes alive for them. History becomes real — and they want to know more! The Grannie Annie provides an opportunity for kids to be inspired by their own family's history.

—Florrie Binford Kichler, Patria Press, www.PatriaPress.com

Taking time away from your technology-filled life to join in The Grannie Annie is like trading fast food for Sunday dinner at Grandma's.

—Debra K. Shatoff, Ed.D., Family therapist and author of *In-Home Child Care: A Step-by-Step Guide to Quality, Affordable Care*

Teachers and parents, if you want to motivate students to love writing, ask them to write for The Grannie Annie.

—Bonnie M. Davis, Ph.D., Author of *How to Teach Students Who Don't Look Like You: Culturally Relevant Teaching Strategies*

Ava Hermann

Christi Fiona

Emily